MARVEL

AT THE MOON

90 DEVOTIONS
YOU'RE NEVER ALONE IN GOD'S MAJESTIC UNIVERSE

LEVI LUSKO

WITH TAMA FORTNER

ILLUSTRATED BY CATHERINE PEARSON
AND TIM BRADFORD

An Imprint of Thomas Nelson

Tommy Nelson, PO Box 141000, Nashville, TN 37214

Published in Nashville, Tennessee, by Tommy Nelson. Tommy Nelson is an imprint of Thomas Nelson. Thomas Nelson is a registered trademark of HarperCollins Christian Publishing, Inc.

Published in association with the literary agency of Wolgemuth & Associates.

Tama Fortner is represented by Cyle Young of C.Y.L.E. (Cyle Young Literary Elite, LLC), a literary agency.

Tommy Nelson titles may be purchased in bulk for educational, business, fund-raising, or sales promotional use. For information, please email SpecialMarkets@ThomasNelson.com.

ISBN 978-1-4002-4269-6 (audiobook)
ISBN 978-1-4002-4268-9 (eBook)

Library of Congress Cataloging-in-Publication Data is on file.

Written by Levi Lusko with Tama Fortner

Illustrated by Catherine Pearson and Tim Bradford

Printed in India

23 24 25 26 27 REP 6 5 4 3 2 1

Mfr: REP / Sonipat, India / August 2023 / PO #12179990

Dedicated to the brave men, women, and families of NASA past, present, and future, whose collective sacrifice allows us to boldly go where no man has gone before and see more of God's majestic universe.

CONTENTS

INTRODUCTION

I LOVE LOOKING UP AT the sky. It's one of my very favorite things to do. I love sunsets and sunrises. I love thunderstorms and clouds shaped like dinosaurs. But I especially love when the Sun goes down because that's when I can see the stars—the twinkling kind and the shooting kind. I can see planets, the dusty glow of the Milky Way, and—brightest of all—the Moon!

Sometimes, when I look up at the Moon, I remember the Bible that's up there. That's right! *There's a Bible on the Moon!* Astronaut Dave Scott left it there in 1971 on one of the last Apollo missions to the Moon. Before he returned to his spacecraft, Scott placed the small red Bible on the control panel of the lunar rover they were leaving behind. (The rover was like a car for driving on the Moon.)

I think about that Bible on summer nights as my family and I spread out blankets on the lawn. We set up our telescope—or pass around binoculars—and stay up late to see God's heavenly show. It's brand-new and different every night. No matter what's going on in my life or in the world, the night sky reminds me of God's power and promises. Sometimes, when bad dreams, fears, or worries wake me up in the night, I go over to my window and look up at the Moon. I remember that God is big enough to create the whole universe, so I know He's big enough to take care of me too. And I feel peace.

King David, who had plenty of tough times, did the same thing. He wrote about it in Psalm 8:3 (ICB):

> I look at the heavens,
> which you made with your hands.
> I see the moon and stars,
> which you created.

The word David used for *hands* actually means "fingers." In other words, God is so mighty that He didn't even need His whole hand to build the skies—just the tips of His fingers! But what's really amazing is that even though God is so huge and powerful, He still cares for us teeny, tiny humans. And that's the main message of *Marvel at the Moon*: You matter to the God who created this whole majestic universe.

As you read through this book, you're going to uncover amazing things about the Moon, how we've explored it, and how we're going to explore it again. You'll be introduced to incredible people and fantastic facts, but most importantly, you'll discover more about Jesus—the One who not only made the Moon but who keeps everything going, on Earth and in the heavens (Colossians 1:16–17)!

I want these ninety devotions to not only launch you into a love of all things space but also to help you see that Jesus is the One who *still* takes giant leaps to rescue you. My prayer is that each devotion you read will help you grow closer to Jesus. His love for you is huge, and He is with you—always!

So, are you ready? All right, then. Countdown to launch activated . . .

Ten. Nine. Eight. Seven. Six. Five. Four. Three. Two. One.

Blastoff!

—Levi

P.S. Speaking of space, be on the lookout! Telescopes are hidden all throughout the illustrations in this book. Why? Because telescopes help us see things we can't see with just our eyes—just like faith helps us see the way God works in our lives, even though we can't see Him. So look carefully! They're different colors and sizes throughout the book. How many can you find? The answers are on page 192.

1

MARVELOUS MOON MAKER

God made the two large lights. He made the brighter light to rule the day. He made the smaller light to rule the night.

GENESIS 1:16 ICB

IF YOU COULD JUMP in a car and drive to the Moon, guess how long it would take you? Almost six months! And that's with no snack breaks! Even though that big, bright full Moon might look like it's close, it's actually about 240,000 miles away from Earth. When you did finally reach the Moon, you'd be in for a bumpy landing. The Moon's surface has been hit by so many meteoroids that it's covered with rocks, a powdery dust made from the bashed-up bits of rock, and huge craters. (One is so big the entire Grand Canyon could fit inside!) Scientists and astronauts (who really did travel to the Moon, but not in a car) have learned a lot about the Moon. But there's one big question they haven't answered: How did the Moon get there?

People have all kinds of theories. Some say it's a piece of Earth that broke off long ago. Others say another planet crashed into Earth and all the rubble lumped together to make the Moon. Some even say Earth stole the Moon from Venus! But I'll tell you what the Bible says. You only have to read a few verses in Genesis 1 before you discover that the Moon had a maker: God. He made the Moon, the Sun, the Earth, and everything in it. And, yeah, He also made you and me. So tonight, look up at the Moon and imagine just how marvelous our God must be!

DID YOU KNOW?

Compared to Earth, the Moon has very little atmosphere or oxygen— that's why it doesn't have blue skies even on the sunniest day. But it does have gravity. It's only about one-sixth as much as Earth's gravity, though. That means you can jump *six times* higher—and slam-dunk a basketball with ease!

GOD, YOU ARE SO AWESOME! YOU MADE THE MOON! NOBODY ELSE COULD EVER DO ANYTHING LIKE THAT. EVERY TIME I SEE IT, I WILL THINK OF YOU AND SAY, "THANKS FOR MAKING ME TOO." AMEN.

2

LOOK UP AT THE STARS

God led Abram outside. God said, "Look at the sky.
There are so many stars you cannot count them. And
your descendants will be too many to count."

GENESIS 15:5 ICB

LONG AGO, GOD TOLD Abram and Sarai that their family would grow into an entire nation. (Imagine a mom and dad having kids who had kids who had kids who had—okay, you get the picture—until their family filled an entire country!) God then told Abram that He would choose that nation to be His very own people. There was just one *huge* problem. Abram and Sarai didn't have any kids! Not a one. And they were really old. Did that stop God? Nope. God told Abram to look up at the night sky. Then He promised that one day Abram's family would outnumber the stars in the sky.

Maybe Abram looked up and started counting. Who wouldn't? But you'd be counting for a *long* time. That's because scientists believe there are more than a hundred billion stars just in our own Milky Way galaxy!

Even after God's promise, Abram didn't have a child right away. Abram and Sarai waited and waited. *For years.* Finally, when they were even older—and God had changed their names to Abraham and Sarah—God kept His promise. (Spoiler alert: He always does!) They had a baby boy named Isaac. Their family grew into the nation of Israel. And it all started with a promise from God. A promise that Abram didn't understand but believed anyway (Genesis 15:6).

Because He is so good, God has also promised us "very great and rich gifts" (2 Peter 1:4 ICB). We might not understand how He'll keep His promises, but we can trust Him to do everything He says He'll do. Just look up at the stars, remember Abram, and believe.

DID YOU KNOW?

If you looked up into a perfectly clear night sky, how many stars would you see? More than two thousand! Add binoculars, and you could see fifty to a hundred thousand. Peek through a two-inch telescope and see more than three hundred thousand. And a sixteen-inch telescope would give you a glimpse of other galaxies—each containing billions of stars! No wonder God wanted Abram to look up at the sky!

GOD, I DON'T ALWAYS UNDERSTAND HOW YOU DO IT, BUT THANK YOU FOR KEEPING YOUR PROMISES. AMEN.

3

A MARVELOUS CHALLENGE

Let us run the race that is before us and never give up.

HEBREWS 12:1 ICB

WORDS CAN CHANGE THE world—or even take us out of this world! That's exactly what happened when President John F. Kennedy gave a speech on September 12, 1962. In that speech, he gave America a goal: send an American to the Moon before the end of 1969.

Here's why: the US was in a great space race with the Soviet Union (now Russia). The Russians had already sent a satellite called Sputnik into space back in 1957. Then, in 1961, Russian cosmonaut Yuri Gagarin became the first human to orbit (or circle) the Earth. America was behind in the race—way behind—and Kennedy announced it was time to catch up and take the lead!

This was a huge—and marvelous—challenge. But check out what Kennedy said: "We choose to go to the Moon in this decade and do the other things, not because they are easy, but because they are hard, . . . because that challenge is one that we are willing to accept."[1]

Choose. Hard. Challenge. Accept. Those are powerful words, and they're the keys to living the best life we can. Because the best life starts when we *choose* to follow God. He's got plans for us—big plans, not boring ones. He might use us to change the world. Or He might use us to change one person's world by helping them find the way to heaven. Sometimes it'll be *hard*, and that's not bad! When we face and *accept* the *challenge* of following God and embrace the difficulty, He'll lead us on adventures greater than anything we could ever imagine—even greater than a trip to the Moon!

GOD, I CHOOSE TO FOLLOW YOU. I KNOW IT MIGHT BE HARD SOMETIMES, BUT PLEASE HELP ME TO ACCEPT THE CHALLENGE! AMEN.

GET READY TO MARVEL!

Challenge yourself with a goal. Maybe it's to memorize a Bible verse—or ten. Maybe it's to make a new friend, run an actual race, write a story, clean your room, or go a whole week without eating sweets. (Okay, that last one might be a little too crazy.) Whatever challenge you choose, write out a mission statement. Here's an example: *I choose to*

_____.

It might be hard, but I accept the challenge. God, please help me do what I can't do on my own.

4

BE LIKE THE MOON

[Jesus] said, "I am the light of the world."

DID YOU KNOW THE Moon doesn't shine? It doesn't even glow. Now, maybe you're thinking, *Sure, then what's that big bright thing in the sky every night?* Okay, yeah, it's the Moon. But it's not actually shining. It's *reflecting*.

Let's try a little demonstration to explain. Grab a small mirror and angle it so the Sun hits it. The mirror gets bright, right? But is the mirror making that light? No. It's *reflecting* it. The Moon does the same thing. It doesn't make its own light. Instead, it acts like a mirror—a gigantic, gray, dusty mirror—that reflects the Sun's light.

John the Baptist was a lot like the Moon. No, he didn't glow or anything like that. He was Jesus' cousin (check out Luke 1–2). John was on a mission to tell the world that the Savior they'd been waiting thousands of years to see was finally coming—Jesus was coming! Even though John was an amazing prophet and teacher and lots of people followed him, he didn't talk about himself. He talked about Jesus. That's because John knew Jesus was the real Light of the World. And his job was to reflect Jesus' light into the world by telling everyone about Him.

Our job is to be like John the Baptist and reflect the light of Jesus into the world too. We do that when we tell others about Him. But we also do that when we love and help others the way Jesus did. That could mean serving meals at a homeless shelter, praying for someone who's sick, helping in Bible class, collecting blankets for foster kids, or being a friend to someone who's lonely. What can you do to reflect His light into the world today?

GOD, HELP ME TO DO AND SAY THE THINGS THAT WILL SHOW OTHERS HOW MUCH JESUS LOVES THEM. I WANT TO SHINE HIS LIGHT! AMEN.

DID YOU KNOW?

To protect their eyes, the Apollo 11 astronauts carried sunglasses on their trip to the Moon. For extra protection, NASA (National Aeronautics and Space Administration) added a special visor on their spacesuit helmets. It blocked out the Sun's strong rays but still let enough light through for the astronauts to see. What made the visor so special? It was coated in a thin layer of actual gold! Talk about expensive shades!

IN THE MIDDLE OF THE MILKY WAY

Trust in him at all times. Pour out your heart to him, for God is our refuge.

PSALM 62:8 NLT

WHAT'S IN THE MIDDLE of the Milky Way galaxy? Well, it's not creamy chocolate and caramel! It's a supermassive black hole formed long, long ago by a dying star. It's named Sagittarius A*. (That * is a symbol meaning "star.") Scientists think Sagittarius A* could be as big as sixteen million miles across. Our own Sun is "only" about 865,000 miles across!

What *is* a black hole? It's an invisible object that forms when stars implode, which means they collapse in on themselves. Some black holes are as small as an atom. (An atom is the super-tiny building block that everything is made

of.) But stellar black holes are up to twenty times the mass of the Sun. (Mass is how much matter is in an object.) And then there are the supermassive black holes that have the mass of one million Suns—or bigger!

The gravity of a black hole is so strong that it pulls in everything around it—even light! Once something gets sucked into a black hole, there's no escape.

Emotions like anger, jealousy, worry, and fear can sometimes feel like a black hole—sucking all the joy and light from our lives. If we let those emotions "explode" out onto the people around us, they can suck away all their joy and light too.

If you're feeling angry, jealous, worried, or afraid, don't explode. And don't stuff your feelings inside and pretend you're not feeling a thing. Tell God everything you're thinking and feeling. You can even tell Him you're upset with Him. God is big enough to handle your biggest and toughest emotions. He'll help you escape them, and He'll pour His light and joy back into your life.

DID YOU KNOW?

Scientists once thought white holes couldn't be real, but now they believe they just might be! White holes are the opposite of black holes. Instead of pulling everything in, white holes don't let anything in. In fact, scientists believe they sometimes "belch" stuff out!

GOD, THANK YOU FOR LETTING ME TALK TO YOU ABOUT EVERYTHING I'M FEELING. I KNOW YOU ARE LISTENING TO ME. AMEN.

INVISIBLE LINES

"If you do good, I will accept you. But if you do not do good, sin is ready to attack you. Sin wants you. But you must rule over it."

GENESIS 4:7 ICB

THERE'S AN INVISIBLE LINE in space. Do you see it? Oh, that's right—it's invisible. But it's still a very important line. It's the Kármán (KAHR-muhn) Line, and it's about sixty-two miles straight up above the Earth. It's the line between the end of the Earth's atmosphere and the beginning of outer space.

Out past the Kármán Line, there's not enough air to breathe. There's not even enough air to scatter the rays of sunlight, which is what makes our sky look blue. That's why outer space looks so black and empty.

Outer space isn't completely empty, though. It's filled with gas and dust particles—they're just *really* spread out. Airplanes fly by pushing down on the particles in our atmosphere to create lift. But above the Kármán Line, there aren't enough particles to lift an airplane. Any craft traveling above the Kármán Line must be ready with some sort of propulsion (pruh-PUHL-shun) system—like jets or rockets—to move safely through space.

Lines can be very helpful. Like the line between right and wrong. God says some things are right, like helping widows and orphans (James 1:27). And God says some things are wrong, like lying (1 Peter 3:10). Choosing right things adds joy and peace to our lives. But choosing wrong things is a sin. It causes all kinds of troubles, and it pulls us away from God and others. Studying God's Word helps us know what's right and what's wrong. Then when we see something wrong or when someone tempts us to do wrong, we'll be ready to draw the line—to walk away, to ask a grown-up for help, or to simply say no. And when you have the courage to draw a line, you help others draw their own lines too.

DID YOU KNOW?

If airplanes can't fly in outer space, why do some spacecraft look like airplanes? The old Space Shuttle and the new Virgin Galactic SpaceShipTwo *do* look a lot like planes. But they still use rockets to launch themselves up into outer space. The wings are only for landing back on Earth.

GOD, PLEASE HELP ME TO KNOW WHAT IS RIGHT AND WHAT IS WRONG. AND HELP ME HAVE THE COURAGE TO CHOOSE WHAT'S RIGHT. AMEN.

HAVE A GOOD TRIP!

"I am the LORD your God, who teaches you what is good for you and leads you along the paths you should follow."

NO AMERICAN HAD EVER ridden a rocket into space *until . . .* 1961, when Alan Shepard climbed into NASA's Mercury spacecraft called the Freedom 7. (NASA is the US government agency that is in charge of the space program.) Shepard was so ready to get into space that when the mission was delayed, he told the NASA guys, "Fix your little problem and light this candle."[2] That candle was the Redstone rocket attached to his spacecraft. When they "lit" it, Shepard and his spacecraft shot up into suborbital (sub-OR-bih-tuhl) space. (That means he reached outer space but wasn't

going fast enough to escape Earth's gravity and get into orbit.) Five minutes later, he reached the highest point of his trip at 116 miles above the Earth. Then the Freedom 7 began dropping back to Earth. It splashed down in the Atlantic Ocean fifteen minutes and twenty-two seconds after it launched.

Today, we send probes to the Sun, crews to the Moon, and rovers to Mars, so Shepard's flight seems like no big deal. But at that time, it was a huge and scary thing. When Shepard's young daughter, Laura, asked him about the trip, he said, "NASA is going to put me into a spacecraft on top of a rocket. The rocket is going to blast me up into space. And I will come back to Earth safely." And you know what Laura said? "OK, have a good trip."[3]

Laura trusted her dad. She didn't ask for all the trip's details or how hard it would be. She trusted her dad to handle it and to do what he said he would do. We can trust our heavenly Dad the same way. We don't have to know every detail of our trip through life. And we don't have to worry whether God is strong enough to handle the troubles we face. He'll do whatever He says He'll do. Because He always does!

DID YOU KNOW?

Alan Shepard had all sorts of survival gear for Freedom 7's return splashdown in the ocean. There were things like food, water, knives, a radio, a first aid kit, matches, a compass, a life vest and raft, and . . . *shark repellent*. Alan could tear open the pouch and pour out the powder to chase sharks away!

GOD, YOU WILL DO EVERYTHING YOU SAY YOU WILL DO. SO I'M GOING TO TRUST YOU WITH ALL THE DETAILS OF MY LIFE'S "TRIP." AMEN.

8 INVENTING MATH?

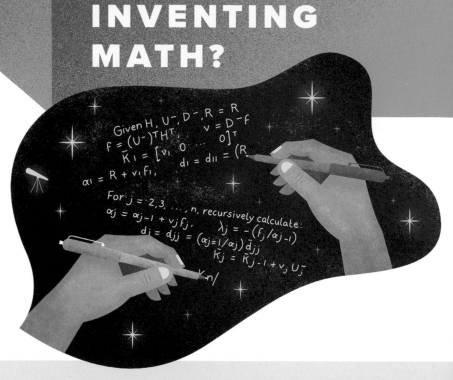

"I will provide for their needs before they ask. I will help them while they are still asking for help."

ISAIAH 65:24 ICB

IN THE 1960S, NASA knew what they wanted to do: launch astronauts into space, land them on the Moon, and get them safely home again. Figuring out how to do that meant solving a whole bunch of math problems. These weren't regular 2 + 2 math problems either. That's because the Earth and Moon are always moving. So you can't aim for where the Moon is right now; you have to aim for where it's going to be. It's like tossing a peach twenty-eight feet in the air and trying to hit just the fuzz with a dart. If you hit the skin, that's a crash landing!

To avoid that crash, NASA needed to invent new ways to solve these new problems. They needed to invent math! (Which is just kind of mind-blowing, right?)

Here's the cool part. Before NASA started asking how to get a man on the Moon, Stanley Schmidt was already working to find the answers. Later, he teamed up with Rudolf Kálmán and developed the Schmidt-Kalman filter. Basically, it made all that complicated new math simple enough for 1960s computers to handle. Their work was a huge part of getting a rocket to the Moon!

NASA figured out some math here and there, but God knows it all! And He can use math to fix some big problems, like when Jesus multiplied a kid's lunch to feed more than five thousand people (John 6). God's control of math—and all things—means He's able to take care of you, no matter what problems come your way. So when you need a new way to solve a problem, trust that God is already working on the answers for you.

GET READY TO MARVEL!

To find more marvelous math in the Bible, look for multiplication in Matthew 18:21–22, some addition in 2 Peter 1:5–7, and lots of crazy subtraction and division in Judges 7. Math matters—even in the Bible. So if you hate math, give it another shot. You might just use it to change the world someday!

GOD, I CAN COUNT ON YOU TO KNOW ALL THE RIGHT ANSWERS—AND TO HELP ME FIND THEM TOO. AMEN.

EASY TO SEE

There are things about God that people cannot see—his eternal power and all the things that make him God. But since the beginning of the world those things have been easy to understand. They are made clear by what God has made.

ROMANS 1:20 ICB

DID YOU KNOW SOME countries have laws against owning a Bible or even talking about Jesus? And many people don't have Bibles to read in their own language. Even in America, some people have never heard a Bible story, met any Christians, or heard about Jesus. So how will these people ever know there is a God?

God made sure everyone can know He is real—through His creation! All we have to do is look up at the Moon, Sun, and stars. Or look around at the people, mountains, and oceans. Because if we really look at them, we'll see how they all work together so perfectly. Like how the Earth has just the right amount of land *and* water for plant and animal life. Like how our planet isn't too close or too far from the Sun. Or how the Moon keeps Earth spinning just right. None of that happened by accident. There had to be a Creator. There has to be a God.

People can know God is real even if they don't know His name or how much He loves them. And when they try to learn more about Him, God promises they will find Him (Jeremiah 29:13). Even in lands where there are no Bibles or other Christians, God is able to show people who He is through dreams or miracles.

If you want to help the world learn who He is, pray for others and tell everyone you meet about Jesus!

DID YOU KNOW?

John Glenn was the first American to orbit the Earth. But that wasn't his last trip to space. He flew again in 1998 at the age of seventy-seven. When he returned to Earth, he told reporters, "To look out at this kind of creation and not believe in God is to me impossible. It just strengthens my faith."[4]

GOD, I WANT EVERYONE TO HAVE A CHANCE TO KNOW YOU. LEAD ME TO PEOPLE I CAN TELL ABOUT JESUS. AMEN.

ZOOMING ALONG

Be kind and loving to each other. Forgive each other just as God forgave you in Christ.

EPHESIANS 4:32 ICB

5 . . . *4* . . . *3* . . . *2* . . . *1* . . . *Ignition. Liftoff!* With those words, astronaut John Glenn and his Mercury spacecraft—nicknamed the Friendship 7—blasted off into space. And America took the lead in the great Space Race with Russia.

Glenn zoomed along at 17,500 miles per hour, reaching 160 miles above the Earth. He circled the Earth *three* times! Glenn spent four hours, fifty-five minutes, and twenty-three seconds in the Friendship 7 before splashing down in the ocean. But his time in the Friendship 7 wasn't all easy. As he headed back toward Earth, Glenn worked hard to keep the spacecraft headed in the right direction. A switch broke, and there were fears that the heat shield might break away—which meant the spacecraft could burn up when it reentered the Earth's atmosphere. But Glenn and his Friendship 7 made it safely home.

Just as Glenn's trip on the Friendship 7 wasn't always easy, our friendships can be tough too. We might be zooming along, having a great time, and then—*bam!* We don't agree. We argue and get upset—even angry! Tempers can burn hot and threaten to explode. And it's easier than ever to hurt each other's feelings.

When you and a friend fight, you might be tempted to call it quits and stop being friends. Instead, take a deep breath and a step back. Talk it through with God. Was it partly—or all—your fault? Do you need to apologize? Or maybe you need to forgive a friend's mistake. Remember, no one's perfect. Not us or our friends. Don't let a fight ruin a good friendship. Because it's when we stick together—when we love and forgive—that we're the best of friends.

DID YOU KNOW?

John Glenn was part of the very first group of astronauts NASA ever picked! Altogether, seven astronauts were chosen for the Mercury space flight program, which is how they got their nickname: the "Mercury Seven." Because the entire nation was fascinated by the Space Race, these men were instantly famous—they even met with President John F. Kennedy!

GOD, HELP ME TO BE A GOOD FRIEND—TO APOLOGIZE AND FORGIVE WHEN I NEED TO. AMEN.

11

UNDER PRESSURE

"I will make you strong and will help you. I will support you with my right hand that saves you."

ISAIAH 41:10 ICB

WHEN ASTRONAUTS BLAST INTO space, the pressure pushing on their bodies is called *g-force*, or gravitational force. It's the same feeling you get on a roller coaster or when an airplane takes off. The force pushes you back into your seat.

G-forces are based on Earth's gravity. Everyone standing on Earth experiences a force of 1 g. When rockets launch, though, astronauts can experience g-forces over 3—and that lasts for several minutes! At 3 g's, some people get dizzy or even pass out! To make sure their astronauts wouldn't pass out, NASA came up with a test: the human centrifuge (SEN-trih-fyooj).

The centrifuge was a giant steel ball at the end of a fifty-foot arm.

Astronauts climbed inside the ball, and a massive four-thousand-horsepower engine spun the arm around and around to create g-forces. (The average car only has about two hundred horsepower!) Astronaut John Glenn dreaded it. *Time* magazine called it a "gruesome merry-go-round."[5] But the centrifuge was important. It told NASA how much g-force pressure an astronaut could take before they passed out.

How much pressure can you take? Not g-forces, but peer pressure—the urge to go along with the crowd—even when you know the crowd is up to no good. We want to fit in, but God tells us we won't fit in perfectly with the world. We're supposed to be different, even if that means people think we're a little weird sometimes (1 Peter 2:9). Standing up to peer pressure isn't easy. On our own, it's practically impossible. That's why God doesn't leave us on our own. He lends us His strength and courage, and He keeps us company when we have to walk away from the crowd. So stick with Him. Because the ultimate g-force is God-Force!

DID YOU KNOW?

When a car zooms from zero to sixty miles per hour, the g-force is about 0.5. Airplane passengers experience g-forces of about 0.4 at takeoff. Many roller coasters have a g-force pull of about 4, though only for a few seconds. But astronauts must stand up to the pressure for several minutes—all while flipping switches, communicating with Mission Control, and piloting through space.

GOD, SOMETIMES OTHER PEOPLE WANT ME TO DO WRONG. HELP ME STAND UP TO THE PRESSURE AND FOLLOW YOU INSTEAD. AMEN.

"THIS IS FUN!"

Every good action and every perfect gift is from God. These good gifts come down from the Creator of the sun, moon, and stars.

JAMES 1:17 ICB

IMAGINE CLIMBING OUT OF a spacecraft and stepping onto . . . *nothing.* No ground, no Earth, no Moon, just space. Look one way, and the Moon glows back at you. Look another way, and the Sun shines bigger and brighter than you've ever seen it before. Far, far below you, the Earth spins with its swirls of blue oceans. And you're just floating right there in the middle of it all. As Ed White said, "This is fun!"[6] Who's Ed White? He was the NASA astronaut who became the first American ever to take a spacewalk when he stepped out of his Gemini 4 spacecraft all the way back in 1965.

Russian Alexei Leonov was the first person ever to step out into space, but he floated for only about ten minutes while "roped" to his spacecraft. White, however, stepped out with a special Hand-Held Maneuvering Unit (HHMU) that looked a lot like a movie-style ray gun. It shot out blasts of oxygen gas and allowed him to steer himself around in space for about twenty-one minutes.

White worked hard—for years and years—to become an astronaut and get to walk in space. But he also knew how important it was to laugh and have fun. After splashing down in the ocean back on Earth, White was pulled out of the water by the crew of the recovery ship, the *Wasp*. He felt so great he even danced a little jig!

It's good to work hard to reach your goals. And it's good to be serious about that work. But it's also important to remember that God created laughter. And it brings us together with Him and with each other in the best of ways. That's probably why He filled this world with so many people and things that make us smile. (Just look at an axolotl [AK-suh-lot-tuhl] or watch an otter play. How could you not smile?) So be serious when it's time to be serious. But also take time to be silly and tell jokes. Get out and play. Do the things you love to do. Hang out with friends. Laugh with your family. And thank God for all the things that make you smile!

DID YOU KNOW?

Ed White loved his spacewalk so much that when NASA radioed that it was time to climb back inside the spacecraft, he joked to his fellow astronaut, James McDivitt, "I'm not coming in." Getting back inside wearing that bulky spacesuit was a slow process. As White climbed back inside the spacecraft, he said, "It's the saddest moment of my life."[7]

GOD, I SEE SO MANY THINGS TO SMILE ABOUT. THANK YOU FOR ALL THE GOOD AND WONDERFUL THINGS YOU'VE CREATED. AMEN.

WHAT HAPPENED TO THE MOON?

There is a right time for everything. Everything on earth has its special season.

ECCLESIASTES 3:1 ICB

WHAT'S UP WITH THE Moon? Some nights it's a huge ball of light. Other nights, it looks like a half-eaten chunk of pie in the sky. Some nights, it's barely a sliver. And then it seems to go away completely. Why does the Moon keep changing its shape? Actually, it doesn't.

The way the Moon orbits the Earth causes us to see more—or less—of it each night. Those changes are called *phases* (FAYZ-ez). Even though the Moon orbits the Earth every 27.3 days, it goes through its phases every 29.5 days because of the way the sunlight hits it.

On day one of the Moon's phases, we see the New Moon—or we might not. That's because the Moon is between Earth and the Sun, blocking the Sun's light. As the Moon continues to orbit the Earth, each night we gradually see more and more of the Sun's reflected light. When the Moon orbits to the opposite side of Earth, we see the entire Moon lit up—the Full Moon. After that night, the Moon begins "shrinking" again.

Like the Moon, your friendships can go through phases. Sometimes you'll be blessed with the best of best friends. Other times, you'll be the new kid in the neighborhood and wondering who you can hang out with. There will be phases when your circle of friends is pretty small. And sometimes your life will be full of friends who care about you. No matter what phase of friendship you're in, you can choose to *be* a friend. Ask God to show you those who are lonely—and invite them into your circle of friends.

GOD, PLEASE HELP ME TO BE A GOOD FRIEND TO THOSE AROUND ME—NO MATTER WHAT PHASE OF FRIENDSHIP I'M IN. AMEN.

DID YOU KNOW?

At the beginning of the Moon's orbit around the Earth, we can barely see it. Then, each night, we see more and more of it. That's called *waxing*. After the Full Moon, we see less and less each night. That's called *waning*. In between are the Gibbous Moon (when we see most but not all of it), Quarter Moon (when it looks like it's split in half), and the Crescent Moon (when it's a crescent-shaped sliver).

14 RAILROADS, ROMANS, AND . . . *ABRAHAM LINCOLN?*

Jesus answered, "I am the way. And I am the truth and the life. The only way to the Father is through me."

JOHN 14:6 ICB

WHAT DO RAILROAD TRACKS, Roman invaders, and Abraham Lincoln have to do with rockets? Check it out! Back in the 1860s, the United States wanted to build a transcontinental railroad to link the West Coast to the East Coast. But first the builders needed to know how wide to make the tracks. President Abraham Lincoln chose the size: four feet, eight and a half inches, the same size as the tram lines in England. And those English tram lines were based on the width of the roads built by Roman invaders over two thousand years ago.

Where do rockets come in? NASA uses builders all around the country to build its rocket parts. So when the rockets and spacecraft for the Space Shuttle missions were being built, they planned to ship all the parts to the launch site in Florida *on railroad tracks*. That meant no one part could be wider than the train or the tunnels they would travel through along the way. And *that's* how a two-thousand-year-old Roman road helped shape the rockets that would journey into the heavens.

Our own journey to heaven was partly shaped by the Romans. It also happened over two thousand years ago, when Jesus was crucified on a Roman cross. When Jesus died, He made a way for our sins to be forgiven. And when He rose again from the grave three days later, He opened wide the path to heaven for us. You can't get there on a railroad or rocket, of course. Jesus is the only way. And you won't need a ticket or a spacesuit. All He asks is that you believe that He is the Savior (Matthew 16:15–17) and obey Him (John 14:15).

DID YOU KNOW?

SpaceX uses semitrucks to ship the pieces of its Falcon 9 rockets from its factories in California to the launching site in Florida. Those parts travel almost 2,500 miles on a special trailer with forty-four wheels! Imagine seeing that as you're riding down the road!

JESUS, YOU ARE THE SON OF GOD. PLEASE TEACH ME HOW TO FOLLOW YOU. AMEN.

UP ABOVE IT ALL

If any of you needs wisdom, you should ask God for it. God is generous. He enjoys giving to all people, so God will give you wisdom.

JAMES 1:5 ICB

SUNRISES? WE SEE THOSE every morning. Moonrises? We can see those most every night if it's not too cloudy. But what about an Earthrise? Only a few people have ever seen one of those.

What is an Earthrise? It's when it looks like the Earth is rising up over the Moon. Why have only a few people seen one? Because you have to be standing on the Moon or be in orbit around it to see this event happen. The first people to see an Earthrise with their own eyes were the astronauts of

Apollo 8: Jim Lovell, Frank Borman, and Bill Anders. On Christmas Eve of 1968, they snapped the legendary picture now called "Earthrise." This picture shows the Earth as a brilliant swirl of blue oceans and white clouds. You can see glimpses of brown and green jungles, forests, and land. The Earth itself seems to hang like a jewel in the velvety black nothingness of space.

Astronauts can see an Earthrise because they're up above it all in space. They have a different view and can see more than we can. That's a little like God. Down here on Earth, we can only see what's right around us. So when things go wrong, it's easy to see only the problems and not the answers. We can feel trapped in a maze of troubles and left on our own to find our way out. But God is up above it all—and at the same time, He's right here with us. (He's God. He can do amazing stuff like that!) Because He sees more than we see, God can see the perfect way out. So ask Him to help you know what to do. He'll happily help you!

LORD, WHEN I DON'T KNOW WHAT TO DO, HELP ME REMEMBER TO ASK YOU! AMEN.

DID YOU KNOW?

That same Christmas Eve, the astronauts sent a television broadcast back to Earth. Their message began at the *very* beginning: "In the beginning God created the heaven and the earth" (Genesis 1:1 KJV). Taking turns, they read Genesis 1:1–10. That night, about a billion people all around the world heard the story of creation. (You can listen too! Just ask your mom or dad to search for "Apollo 8 Christmas broadcast" on YouTube.)

16
THE DARK SIDE

Lord, you have examined me. You know all about
me. You know when I sit down and when I get up.
You know my thoughts before I think them.

PSALM 139:1–2 ICB

THE DARK SIDE. (IT sounds even cooler if you read it in Darth
Vader's voice!) But I'm not talking about movies here. I'm talking
about the Moon. The dark side of the Moon is the side we can't see
from Earth. But in 1968, Frank Borman, Jim Lovell, and Bill Anders were cruising along in their Apollo 8 spacecraft when they became the first people

to *ever* see the dark side of the Moon with their own eyes.

It isn't really the "dark" side, though. It's more like the "far" side. You see, the Moon rotates and has days and nights just like Earth. But because it rotates at the same rate that it circles around the Earth, we see only one side of it. Confusing? Let me explain. Imagine a friend is standing still while you run in a circle around them. As you run, you turn so that you're always facing them. They never see your back. That's what happens with the Moon and Earth.

Like the Moon, a lot of us keep part of ourselves hidden from the world. Usually it's the part that makes us unique. And usually it's because we're worried about what others will think. We're afraid they'll laugh at our love of painting or that they'll make fun of just how many space facts we know. But so what if they do? God made us to be unique. Don't hide those parts away. Use them to tell the world how awesome our God is!

GET READY TO MARVEL!

Let's face it. We're all a little weird, and that's okay. God made each of us unique (Psalm 139:13–14). Spend some time today doing that "weird" thing you love. Jump on your skateboard. Dive into a book. Grab your paints. Play your trombone. Do the splits. Head out for a hike. Stare up at the stars. Dare to be wonderful, marvelous you!

GOD, HELP ME TO SEE THE UNIQUE PARTS OF ME AS GOOD AND WONDERFUL. AND HELP ME TO SEE THAT OTHERS ARE UNIQUE IN WONDERFUL WAYS TOO. AMEN.

ALL ON A MISSION!

**All of you together are the body of Christ.
Each one of you is a part of that body.**

1 CORINTHIANS 12:27 ICB

THERE'S NO WAY A *person can land on the Moon!* That's what some people said. But the Apollo 11 mission proved it could be done. Everything about that mission was special, right down to the patch that went on the flight suits, jackets, and gear. It was designed by the astronauts themselves: Neil Armstrong, Buzz Aldrin, and Michael Collins.

Of course, the mission's name was placed at the top. The small blue marble of Earth is in the background, and the eagle represents the United

States. See that thing the eagle is carrying? It's an olive branch—a symbol of peace. It was a message to the world that Apollo 11 was all about peaceful exploration.

The coolest part, though, is what *isn't* on the patch: the astronauts' names. They knew they didn't make this mission happen by themselves. Over four hundred thousand engineers, scientists, mathematicians, secretaries, janitors, and more worked together to make Apollo 11 possible. Since all those names wouldn't fit on the patch, the astronauts didn't want their names on it either.

That's how God's family should be too. We're *all* on a mission of peace to tell the world about Jesus. No one person can do it all on their own, *and* no one person ever has to do it all on their own. We help each other, cheer for each other, and encourage each other. It's not about getting famous or getting glory for ourselves. It's about sharing the good news about the One who died to save us. So the only name on our mission patch should be His: *Jesus*!

JESUS, YOU'VE GIVEN ME A MISSION TO TELL THE WORLD ABOUT YOU. HELP ME REMEMBER THE MISSION IS ABOUT YOU, NOT ME. AMEN.

DID YOU KNOW?

Neil Armstrong and Buzz Aldrin left a few things behind on the Moon: a disc containing messages from seventy-three world leaders, including England's Queen Elizabeth II; an American flag; a patch honoring the lives lost on Apollo 1; and a plaque. The plaque says, "Here men from the planet Earth first set foot upon the moon. July 1969 A.D. We came in peace for all mankind."[8] If you could choose just one thing to leave on the Moon for future missions to find, what would it be?

18

HOW'S THE AIR UP THERE?

The sky was made at the Lord's command. By the breath from his mouth, he made all the stars.

PSALM 33:6 ICB

IF YOU PLAN ON taking a trip to the Moon, don't forget your spacesuit! You're going to need its oxygen tanks to breathe. That's because the atmosphere of the Moon is very different from Earth's. Our atmosphere is made up of layers and has plenty of oxygen. But the Moon's atmosphere has just one thin layer. And its gravity isn't strong enough to hold even that one layer of atmosphere close to its surface, like Earth's gravity does. Plus, solar winds blow through and spread it out even more.

Earth's atmosphere has about twenty-seven quintillion molecules in every cubic centimeter. (That's a space about the size of a pencil eraser.) But the Moon's atmosphere has only about a hundred molecules in a cubic centimeter. It has helium, neon, argon, and hydrogen gases but practically no oxygen. So without a spacesuit, you can't breathe on the Moon!

Sometimes it can be tough to breathe right here on Earth. It can happen when you're afraid, angry, or just plain stressed out. You might breathe hard or have trouble catching your breath. If that happens, try *box breathing*. Close your eyes and use your finger to draw a square (or box) in the air. As you draw one side, slowly breathe in as you count to four. Then, breathe out slowly as you count to four again and draw the next side. Keep drawing sides of the box until you feel calmer. Then quietly whisper a prayer to God about whatever is upsetting or stressing you. His peace will fill you up like the air that you breathe (Philippians 4:7).

DID YOU KNOW?

Astronauts say space smells like hot metal, truck fumes, barbecue, or even burnt toast. No, they don't take off their helmets to take a sniff. But when they step back inside their spacecraft after a spacewalk, the scent sticks to their suits. NASA once had a perfume maker recreate the smell for training astronauts. You can buy a bottle for yourself! Warning: it's kind of stinky!

GOD, WHEN I'M UPSET OR STRESSED OUT, REMIND ME THAT YOU ARE HERE. PLEASE GIVE ME YOUR PEACE THAT PASSES UNDERSTANDING SO THAT I CAN BREATHE. AMEN.

TRAILBLAZER

**"See, I am doing a new thing! . . . I am making a way
in the wilderness and streams in the wasteland."**

ISAIAH 43:19 NIV

A *TRAILBLAZER* CARVES OUT A trail, or path, for others to follow. You might imagine someone hacking their way through the wilderness. But Katherine Johnson blazed a trail through the world of math and rocket science—all the way to the Moon!

In the 1950s, when Katherine began working for NASA, very few women or people of color worked in math and science. It was a time of segregation (seh-grih-GAY-shuhn) when Black people were separated from White people and

weren't given the same rights. Back then, NASA wanted to launch the first American into space. They needed to know when and where the rocket should launch so that it landed at just the right time and place. They couldn't figure it out, but Katherine did!

Katherine also worked on other NASA missions, including Apollo 11 and the Space Shuttle. Her math is even being used in the Artemis missions to the Moon!

Katherine's work blazed a trail through NASA for other women and minorities to follow. But there's an even more amazing trailblazer: *Jesus.*

When Jesus came to Earth, He carved out a path for us by showing us how to love God and live the right way. And when He died and rose again, He cut a path through sin and death. That path leads us straight to God! The best part is, Jesus doesn't expect us to follow His path alone. He walks with us every step of the way!

LORD, THANK YOU SO MUCH FOR SENDING JESUS TO BLAZE A TRAIL TO HEAVEN FOR ME TO FOLLOW. SHOW ME HOW I CAN HELP OTHERS FOLLOW HIS TRAIL TOO. AMEN.

DID YOU KNOW?

Human computer. That's what NASA called Katherine Johnson and the others who did NASA's math by hand. Katherine was such a genius with math that astronaut John Glenn refused to get in his spacecraft until she double-checked the computer's math. Katherine did, the numbers matched, and Glenn said, "If she says they're good, then I'm ready to go."[9] Glenn then blasted off to become the first American to circle the Earth.

20

WHAT TIME IS IT?

Use every chance you have for doing good.

EPHESIANS 5:16 ICB

IF YOU WANT TO know what time it is, that's easy to answer. You can just look at a clock. Even finding out what time it is in India isn't too tough. You can ask a parent to help you look it up on the internet. But in space? Figuring out the time isn't so easy!

That's because our clocks and time here on Earth are linked to how long it takes the Earth to go around the Sun—365.24 days. But when you're hundreds of thousands of miles away from Earth, what do astronauts do? They use MET, or Mission Elapsed (ih-LAPSD) Time. (*Elapsed* means how much time has passed.)

The second the rocket boosters ignite, MET begins. Before that point, NASA uses a countdown clock. It starts counting down forty-three hours before the launch. When it reaches zero—and the rocket boosters fire—MET time begins counting forward. It records hours, minutes, and seconds. For example, Apollo 11's Lunar Module (LOO-ner MOJ-ool) landed on the Moon at 102 hours, 45 minutes, and 40 seconds. In MET, that would be written as 102:45:40.

No matter how we count time, every moment is a gift from God. And we don't want to waste a second of His gift! Not on scrolling through screens. Not on trying to get more and more stuff. Not on being worried or upset about what others think. Instead, let's choose to make the most of the moments God has given us. Talk to people. Talk to them *about Him*. Love, care, and help. Explore and learn. Go on adventures and do good things for yourself, for others, and for God. That's the mission of life!

DID YOU KNOW?

NASA's switch from counting down to counting forward is almost like time starting over. That also happened when Jesus came to Earth. The years before Jesus was born are called *BC* (before Christ). And the years after His birth are called *AD*, which stands for anno Domini. That's Latin for "in the year of our Lord."

GOD, YOU'VE GOT A MISSION PLANNED FOR ME TODAY. PLEASE HELP ME TO COMPLETE MY MISSION AND NOT WASTE A SECOND. AMEN.

WHEN TIMES GET TOUGH

"In this world you will have trouble. But be brave! I have defeated the world!"

JOHN 16:33 ICB

TEST PILOT. ASTRONAUT. FIRST man to walk on the Moon. Neil Armstrong had an amazing and adventure-filled career—and it was all about flying. That's because Neil Armstrong loved to fly. From the time he was six years old and took his first airplane ride, he couldn't get enough of airplanes. He read about them, studied them, and built models of them. And as he grew up, he learned to fly them. Then one day, he got the chance to fly all the way to the Moon!

Armstrong will be remembered forever as the first man to walk on the Moon. But his life wasn't all success, good times, and happiness. He had struggles too. Some were little, and some were huge—like when his young daughter passed away.

In this life, we're all going to have wonderful, good, and happy times. But we're also going to have tough and lonely times. Because sometimes friends move away. We mess up, or other people mess up. Natural disasters tear up homes and schools. And we may lose people we care about. Yes, struggles and sadness happen in this world. But what matters most is what we do when those hard times happen.

When you're hit with a hard time, reach out to someone who's been through what you're going through. It can be helpful to talk about the sadness you are feeling, particularly with a trusted adult like a parent, teacher, or counselor. And most of all, let God comfort you. You can talk to Him—He's the best listener ever! Or you can simply sit with Him. You don't have to say a word because He knows everything and understands just what you're going through. After all, Jesus went through some tough and terrible times in this world too. Those troubles didn't stop Him, and He won't let your troubles stop you from doing all that He created you to do!

GET READY TO MARVEL!

It helps to remember happy times when you're going through a tough time. So start a memory collection. Gather pictures, write down stories, and make drawings of happy memories that make you smile. Collect them in a journal or scrapbook. When you're feeling lonely or sad, pull them out and let all those marvelous memories remind you of all the reasons you have to smile.

GOD, WHEN LIFE IS HARD, HELP ME REMEMBER TO REACH OUT TO YOU. AMEN.

22

EVERYBODY IS CIRCLING

"The thing you should want most is God's kingdom and doing what God wants. Then all these other things you need will be given to you."

MATTHEW 6:33 ICB

IF THE SUN IS a star and the Earth is a planet, then what is the Moon? Well, our Moon is actually . . . a moon. Its name *is* what it is. It would be like naming your dog *Dog*. Not very creative, huh? Okay, let's dig a little deeper.

Scientifically speaking, the Moon is a *natural satellite*. That's an object in space that orbits another object. Okay . . . but the Earth orbits the Sun, so why is it a planet instead of a moon? The difference is that planets orbit a star—like how the Earth circles the Sun. But moons orbit a planet—like how the Moon circles Earth.

And why is our Moon called *the Moon*? (After all, we don't live on *the Planet* and orbit *the Star*!) It's because the ancient astronomers—or space scientists—who named it didn't know other planets had moons too. They thought our Moon was the only one!

Like the Moon, we all circle something. That is, we all put something at the center of our lives, something that's most important to us. For some of us, that's being popular. The problem is, what it takes to be popular is always changing. We might even be expected to do things that are wrong just to stay popular—like gossip or be mean to others. And we can end up caring more about what the popular kids say than what God says.

So make sure that Jesus is at the center of your life. Circle around Him. Because He never changes. He never asks you to do what's wrong. And what He says about you is good and true.

GOD, PLEASE TEACH ME HOW TO MAKE YOU THE CENTER OF MY LIFE. I WANT TO LIVE MY WHOLE LIFE CIRCLING AROUND YOU. AMEN.

DID YOU KNOW?

We are learning new things about the universe all the time, but there's still so much we don't know. For example, Pluto, a dwarf planet, was discovered in 1930. But it wasn't until 1978 that we found out it has a moon! Two more moons were found in 2005, another in 2011, and another in 2012. Then, in 2015, we discovered Pluto has ice volcanoes!

23

ALREADY THERE

The Lord is close to everyone who prays to him, to all who truly pray to him.

PSALM 145:18 ICB

THE FASTEST PERSON ON Earth can run just over twenty-seven miles per hour. The fastest horse has been clocked at fifty-five miles per hour. And the fastest car can race along at over three hundred miles per hour. But all three are like turtles slow-poking across the street compared to Apollo 11.

On its trip to the Moon, the Apollo 11 rocketed along at speeds that sometimes reached as high as twenty-five thousand miles per hour. That's over 416 miles every minute—or almost seven miles a second. That's more than ten times as fast as a bullet. Good thing there are no speeding tickets in space! Apollo 11 didn't travel that fast all the time. After it escaped the Earth's atmosphere, it cruised along for much of the time at *only* about 2,040 miles per hour. Even going that fast, it took the Apollo 11 spacecraft three days, three hours, and forty-nine minutes to reach the Moon. Why did it take so long? Because the Moon is about 240,000 miles away!

Even though the Moon, Sun, and stars are far, far away, the One who made them isn't. And we don't have to speed into outer space to be with Him. That's because when we decide we want to follow God—to live our lives loving Him and others—we become part of His family. His own children! And He is the best, most perfect Dad ever! He's never too busy to listen and always has time to talk. In fact, whenever you need God—or whenever you just want to hang out—He doesn't need to come running to you. Because He's already there.

DID YOU KNOW?

The fastest ever trip to the Moon was also the very first (sort of) successful one. The unmanned Russian Luna 2 crash-landed on the Moon in 1959 just thirty-six hours after its launch. A few months before, the Luna 1 had been on track to make an even faster trip. But it was traveling so fast that it zipped right past the Moon and zoomed off into space!

LORD, THANK YOU FOR STAYING SO CLOSE TO ME. I NEVER HAVE TO WONDER WHERE YOU ARE BECAUSE YOU ARE ALWAYS HERE WITH ME. AMEN.

24

WHO ARE YOU LISTENING TO?

For our high priest is able to understand our weaknesses. He was tempted in every way that we are, but he did not sin.

HEBREWS 4:15 ICB

WHAT DID YOU SAY? *Who said that?* That's what the astronauts of Apollo 11—and every other space mission—would have been saying if they hadn't had a CapCom.

That's because, while there were only three men on Apollo 11, Mission Control back on Earth was filled with people. Some made sure the spacecraft stayed on the right course. The flight surgeon kept an eye on the astronauts' health. Others handled computer issues. All those people working together meant lots and lots of talking. The astronauts couldn't possibly listen to them all!

That's where the CapCom (short for Capsule Communicator) came in. The CapCom listened to everyone and then told the astronauts just what they needed to know. The CapCom was the *only* voice the astronauts listened to. For Apollo 11, four fellow astronauts at Mission Control took turns being the CapCom. Because they had gone through the same astronaut training as the Apollo 11 crew, they knew every step of the mission. The crew trusted these four men to understand what the crew was going through.

You have lots of voices talking around you too. On the internet and social media. At home and school. These voices can say very different things. You need one voice to listen to. Someone who's been where you've been. Someone who can tell you just what you need to know. You need a CapCom. And you have one: Jesus! He lived on Earth and was a kid once too. He's been through everything you're going through. He got hungry, sad, and lonely. He was tempted to do wrong. He even got separated from His parents on a trip! So you can trust Jesus to understand. He's the one Voice you should always listen to.

LORD, HELP ME LISTEN TO YOUR VOICE. AMEN.

GET READY TO MARVEL!

Grab a friend and pretend you're on a Moon mission! One of you be the CapCom at Mission Control, while the other is an astronaut up on the Moon's Tranquility Base (behind a chair or the couch). Talk to each other using walkie-talkies if you have them—or make your own from decorated toilet paper rolls. Then take huge, bouncy Moon steps out to the kitchen for a snack. After all, Moon missions can make you hungry!

25

BEFORE YOU NEED IT

Keep my words and store up my commands within you. . . . Write them on the tablet of your heart.

PROVERBS 7:1, 3 NIV

SEVEN AND A HALF minutes. That's how close Neil Armstrong and Buzz Aldrin were to landing on the Moon. And *that's* when the alarm went off.

Armstrong was the pilot in charge of getting the Lunar Module down to the Moon's surface. It was tricky, and he couldn't see exactly where he was going. Suddenly an alarm screamed through the small spacecraft. (It would be like a fire alarm going off in your closet!) An error code flashed up on the computer screen: 1202. The astronauts had seen lots of error codes in training, but not this one. Would they have to call off the mission? Would they crash?

Back on Earth, NASA engineers scrambled to find the answer. But one engineer, John "Jack" Garman, already knew it. Long before Apollo 11 ever launched, he wrote every possible computer error code on a piece of paper, just in case. So Garman knew what 1202 meant—the computer was trying to do too many things at once. It would fix itself! The CapCom (see page 56) called out, "We're go on that alarm"—which meant the mission could continue.[10]

Garman had the answer *before* he needed it, and you can too. Maybe not to computer problems, but to the problems of life. The answers are in God's Word. So *before* problems come up, write His Word on your heart. Not with a pen, but by reading it, thinking about it, and memorizing it. Then, when problems, fears, and other alarms blast at you, you'll already know what God wants you to do. Like when you're tempted to get even with someone who's hurt your feelings, you can remember 1 Peter 3:9. Check it out!

GOD, THANK YOU FOR THE ANSWERS IN YOUR WORD. HELP ME TO WRITE THEM ON MY HEART AND MIND. AMEN.

GET READY TO MARVEL!

Want a super-easy way to write a verse on your heart? Try this: Write a Bible verse on paper and read it aloud. Then, erase or cover up one word, and read the verse again. Do you remember the missing word? Erase another word, then another and another— until you have the whole verse memorized.
Hint: John 11:35 and 1 Thessalonians 5:16 are great ones to start with. Look them up to see why!

26

DON'T WORRY?

Do not worry about anything. But pray and ask God for everything you need. And when you pray, always give thanks.

PHILIPPIANS 4:6 ICB

THE SEA OF TRANQUILITY (tran-KWIL-ih-tee) was the spot on the Moon where the Apollo 11 Lunar Module was supposed to land. Except this sea didn't have any water, and the landing wasn't tranquil—or peaceful—at all!

NASA chose the Sea of Tranquility because it was a smooth, dry plain. But as the Lunar Module neared the Moon's surface, Neil Armstrong realized they were off course and about to land in a crater piled with huge boulders. Some were as big as cars! *Not good!* Armstrong took control and steered the module to a smoother spot—all while a computer alarm screeched in his ears. (Check out page 58 to learn why.) He managed to land with only about forty-five seconds worth of fuel left. *Whew!*

Later, Armstrong said that landing was the hardest part of the whole mission. There were so many things they didn't know and "a thousand things to worry about."[11]

Hmmm . . . so many things we don't know? A thousand things to worry about? Sounds like an ordinary day here on Earth! Just when we think we've got stuff figured out—like friendships, where to sit in the lunchroom, and how to do long division—everything changes! Friends move or get all dramatic about who you sit with at lunch. Long division turns into fractions. The Bible says not to worry, but how?

Here's how: pray! Pray about everything that's worrying you. Pray about all those "boulders" blocking your path. And then? Thank God—because you can believe He's going to either blast those boulders out of your way or steer you safely through them.

LORD, THERE ARE SO MANY THINGS I DON'T KNOW, BUT YOU KNOW ALL THINGS, INCLUDING HOW TO TAKE CARE OF ME. AMEN.

GET READY TO MARVEL!

Armstrong called the spot where they landed *Tranquility Base*. It was a place to rest for a while after a tough landing. We all need a place like that. So make your own! Choose a peaceful spot—a swing, a bedroom corner or closet, or even a treehouse. (A backyard firepit is a really cool spot too.) When worries grab you, head for your tranquility base and let God help you sort things through.

27

THINK NEW THOUGHTS

**Do not be shaped by this world. Instead be
changed within by a new way of thinking.**

ROMANS 12:2 ICB

THE WEIRDEST LOOKING CONTRAPTION I have ever seen
in the sky." That's what astronaut Michael Collins called the Apollo
11 Lunar Module (also known as the LM or the Eagle).[12] The LM didn't
look like a plane or a rocket. And even though it was named after a bird, the
crew thought it looked more like a weird, alien bug!

Because the LM would do things no spacecraft had done before, engineers
needed to get creative. They made it boxy to help it balance on the unknown
surface of the Moon. Gold foil covered parts of it to keep temperatures safe for

the astronauts. And those spindly legs? They folded up when the LM was attached to the main spacecraft and unfolded for landing on the Moon. To keep the spacecraft light, the LM didn't have seats. Astronauts flew standing up using a new invention—Velcro—to anchor their shoes to the spacecraft's floor.

The LM might have looked weird, but of the ten modules flown into space, not one of them failed. (Aquarius, the Apollo 13 LM, even served as the "life raft" for the crew and saved their lives!)

The LM engineers had to think of new ways to do things. That's something God gave each of us the ability to do—think new thoughts. That means you're not stuck thinking the same old thoughts or doing the same old things. For example, if you happen to find yourself alone for the afternoon, you don't have to feel lonely or fill up the day watching videos. Instead, you can dream up ways to have fun by yourself. Invent a new game. Imagine a story. Write a letter to God. Create a work of art. Let your mind think of something new to do!

DID YOU KNOW?

Woohoo! Hooray! We made it! What would you say if you'd just landed on the Moon? Neil Armstrong said, "Houston, Tranquility Base here. The Eagle has landed."[13] Neil said "Houston" because that was NASA's base on Earth. Tranquility Base was what they called the place where they landed. And the Eagle was the name of the Lunar Module.

LORD, YOU GAVE ME AN AMAZING BRAIN. HELP ME USE IT TO THINK OF NEW WAYS TO SHOW HOW MUCH I LOVE YOU. AMEN.

ALL THE WAY UP ON THE MOON

"I am the vine, and you are the branches. If a person remains in me and I remain in him, then he produces much fruit. But without me he can do nothing."

JOHN 15:5 ICB

ON JULY 20, 1969, THE Apollo 11 Lunar Module separated and pulled away from the main spacecraft, where astronaut Michael Collins stayed. The module—called the Eagle—was a mini-spacecraft specially designed for landing on the Moon. Inside were the other two astronauts: Buzz Aldrin and Neil Armstrong. After two hours of careful steering, the Eagle landed. For the first time in the history of our world, people were on the Moon!

If you landed on the Moon, wouldn't you want to jump out and start exploring right away? But NASA told the astronauts to wait. They needed to check the systems and set the controls. Then, before they put on life support gear and stepped outside, Buzz Aldrin chose to remember the One who made the Moon. He read the words of John 15:5 and took communion. (Maybe it should be called kuh-*MOON*-yuhn. Get it?)

Communion is a special meal eaten to remember what Jesus did for us on the cross. Those who follow Him eat a small piece of bread to remember the way Jesus' body was broken for us. Then we drink a little wine or grape juice to remember the blood He shed to pay for our sins. We do these things because Jesus asked us to remember Him and never forget (Luke 22:19–20). That's why Buzz took communion, but he also did it to remember that God was there with him. All the way up on the Moon. Because no matter where we go— even to infinity and beyond—God is with us.

DID YOU KNOW?

Jesus took the first communion at the Last Supper, which is the name of the last meal Jesus shared with His disciples before He went to the cross. That means the Last Supper was also the *first* meal eaten on the Moon. Pretty marvelous, right? (Read more about the Last Supper in Luke 22:7–38.)

GOD, HELP ME NEVER DOUBT YOUR LOVE SINCE YOU WERE WILLING TO SEND JESUS TO DIE FOR ME. I LOVE YOU TOO. AMEN.

NOT SMALL AT ALL

"I have called you by name, and you are mine."

ISAIAH 43:1 ICB

IMAGINE BEING ABLE TO fly an airplane before you even get your driver's license! That's what Neil Armstrong did. When he was only six years old, his dad took him flying for the first time—and he was hooked. His love for all things aircraft and space was born.

Armstrong studied hard and became a research pilot for NASA. He flew more than two hundred different kinds of aircraft, including jets, helicopters, gliders, and rockets. In 1962, he became an astronaut, and the skies suddenly

got a whole lot bigger for him. Armstrong took his first trip into space in 1966 as the command pilot of the Gemini 8, where he had to use his quick thinking to keep things from spinning out of control.

But his most famous trip happened on July 20, 1969. That's when Neil Armstrong became the first person *ever* to set foot on the Moon. (His left foot touched first, just in case you were wondering.) As the first person to see Earth from the Moon, Armstrong said, "It suddenly struck me that that tiny pea, pretty and blue, was the Earth. I put up my thumb and shut one eye, and my thumb blotted out the planet Earth. I didn't feel like a giant. I felt very, very small."[14]

Give it a try but in reverse. Look up at the night sky and hold out your thumb. Can you blot out the Moon? When we look up at the endlessness of space, it can make us feel pretty small. But the God who created all that—who created everything—knows *your* name. He can even say it and spell it the right way. You're not small at all, and you're endlessly important to Him!

DID YOU KNOW?

Neil Armstrong wasn't the only person to walk around on the Moon that day. Buzz Aldrin took a stroll up there too. And those footprints they left behind? They're still there. In fact, they'll be there for the next million years or so because there's no wind on the Moon to blow them away!

GOD, YOU ARE SO HUGE AND SO POWERFUL, BUT YOU STILL CHOOSE TO KNOW ME. THAT'S JUST AMAZING. THANK YOU! AMEN.

30 CHOOSING TO CELEBRATE

Be happy with those who are happy.

ROMANS 12:15 ICB

NINETEEN MINUTES AFTER NEIL Armstrong became the first man to walk on the Moon, Buzz Aldrin became the second.

That Apollo 11 mission was Buzz's first trip to the Moon but *not* his first trip into space. Three years before, in 1966, he traveled into space on the Gemini 12 mission. One of that mission's goals was to prove men could safely work in space—and Buzz did it! He went on three different spacewalks (that's anytime an astronaut steps outside the spacecraft). Buzz spent a record-breaking five hours and forty-eight minutes outside his spacecraft. He even took a selfie—the first selfie from space!

Despite his amazing firsts, Buzz is most famous for being the *second* person to walk on the Moon. As cool as that was, some people say it's not as amazing as being first. It would've been easy for someone like Buzz to get jealous or even angry.

But here's the thing: someone has to be first, and it can't always be us. So what do we do when someone else wins, outscores us, or gets the thing we want? It's easy to be jealous, stomp our feet, or throw a fit. But what good does that really do? Jealousy only causes problems—like hurt feelings, anger, and a sad end to what might have been a fun game, day, or sleepover.

Instead, let's choose to celebrate with those who win. Like Romans 12:15 says, "Be happy with those who are happy" (ICB). Why? Because everyone needs a chance to shine. One day, it will be your turn. But until then, cheer the winners on!

GOD, HELP ME TO BE THANKFUL FOR WHAT I HAVE AND BE HAPPY FOR THE PERSON WHO GOT WHAT I WANTED. I KNOW THAT ONE DAY YOU'LL HELP ME SHINE TOO. AMEN.

DID YOU KNOW?

Where does a name like *Buzz* come from? A little sister! Buzz's parents named him Edwin Eugene Aldrin Jr. But when his little sister tried to say "brother," it kept coming out as "buzzer." The family shortened it to Buzz, and the rest is history! Years later, *Toy Story* writers honored the astronaut by naming one of the characters Buzz Lightyear. Who would have guessed a mispronounced nickname would lead to infinity and beyond?

31

BUSY WHILE YOU WAIT

Wait for the Lord's help and follow him.

PSALM 37:34 ICB

THE MOON DOES MORE than just sit up in the sky. It's busy up there! It lights up the night—even when it's just a sliver! Then there's the whole gravity thing. The Moon's pull keeps the Earth perfectly tilted at 23.5 degrees. If the Moon disappeared, that tilt would change. The Earth might wobble, and that wobble would change our seasons. Winter could get colder and summer hotter. Or there might be no seasons at all!

The Moon's pull on the Earth also slows down its rotation, or spin. Without the Moon, the Earth would spin so fast that a day would last only six to twelve hours instead of twenty-four. And a year would last longer than a thousand days—you'd have to wait *forever* for your next birthday!

While it's nice not waiting a thousand days for your birthday, we do have to wait sometimes—like waiting for our turn. There are times we even have to wait on God. Yes, He promises to answer our prayers (Psalm 91:15), but sometimes His answer is "wait." Though it might feel like He's not doing anything, God is busy behind the scenes, working everything out (Romans 8:28). For example, you might ask God to send a new friend when your best friend moves away. Instead of plopping a new pal right in front of you, though, God might spend some time teaching you how to be a good friend to those already around you, or He might open your eyes to see someone in your life you have overlooked.

What should you do while you wait? Be busy too. Keep doing the things you know are right. Be kind and helpful. Talk to God. Read His Word. Keep loving Him and loving others. Don't sit around doing nothing. Be busy while you wait.

GOD, YOU KNOW THE PERFECT TIME AND WAY TO ANSWER MY PRAYERS. HELP ME STAY BUSY LOVING AND SERVING YOU WHILE I WAIT. AMEN.

DID YOU KNOW?

Regular ink pens need gravity to pull the ink "down," so they don't work in space. Pencils work, but tiny flecks of lead break off and float around the spacecraft. And that's dangerous! So in 1965, the Fisher Pen Company invented the space pen. Its special, pressurized ink cartridge lets it write upside down, in extreme heat and cold, underwater, and in space. To keep them from floating away, astronauts wrap the pens in Velcro and stick them to the walls!

32

NEVER, EVER ALONE

"The Lord your God is with you. The mighty One will save you."

ZEPHANIAH 3:17 ICB

NO ONE IN THE history of the entire world has ever been more alone than Michael Collins. Here's how it happened.

When the Apollo 11 spacecraft took off, three astronauts were on board: Michael Collins, Neil Armstrong, and Buzz Aldrin. After reaching orbit around the Moon, their spacecraft separated into two pieces: the Eagle Lunar Module and the Columbia Command Module. The Eagle headed for the Moon's surface with Armstrong and Aldrin inside. But Collins stayed behind in the Columbia, piloting it around the Moon and waiting for the Eagle to return.

For the next twenty-one hours, Collins was completely alone in space while Armstrong and Aldrin were sixty-five miles below him on the Moon.

Every two hours, Collins orbited the Moon. Part of that time, he could talk to NASA and the other astronauts. But when he traveled to the Moon's far side, there was only silence—and a gigantic hunk of rock between him and every other person in the universe.

Though it seemed like Collins was all alone, he wasn't. God was with him even on the far side of the Moon. Because God is everywhere.

If you grow up to be an astronaut and zoom off to Mars or Pluto or beyond, God will be there. In fact, there's no place you'll *ever* go where God will not be with you. Not the doctor's office, not the lunchroom, not the basketball tryouts. God is everywhere and always watching over you. Read Psalm 139, and you'll see that God is not someone you want to play hide-and-seek with. You can't hide from Him no matter where you go! (Just check out Jonah 1–2 to find out about that whole fish thing when Jonah tried to run away from God!)

GOD, WHEN I'M FEELING ALONE, REMIND ME THAT YOU ARE ALWAYS WITH ME. AMEN.

GET READY TO MARVEL!

Being by yourself can actually be amazing! After all, you like all the same stuff as you. You have the same favorite snacks. You even laugh at the same jokes! So spend a little time alone today. Make friends with yourself and enjoy hanging out with just you. And while you do, talk to God. After all, He's there with you too, which is really good to remember when you're feeling lonely at school or feeling worried while trying to sleep.

33

TASK ACCOMPLISHED

"Go and make followers of all people in the world. Baptize them in the name of the Father and the Son and the Holy Spirit."

MATTHEW 28:19 ICB

A **MERICA WON THE GREAT** Space Race! With Apollo 11, America became the first nation to put a man on the Moon. Back at Mission Control in Houston, everyone gathered for the astronauts' return. They watched as the capsule carrying the three astronauts splashed down in the Pacific Ocean. They waited as the ship assigned to pick up the astronauts, the *USS Hornet,* plowed through the waters toward the splashdown site. They watched as the recovery team pulled the astronauts on board the ship. And then they celebrated!

The words of President John F. Kennedy's challenge to land a man on the

Moon flashed up on the screen at Mission Control. On another screen, a picture of the Apollo 11 mission patch appeared with the words "Task Accomplished, July 1969." NASA had accomplished everything they had set out to do.

When Jesus finished His mission here on Earth, He didn't say, "Task accomplished." Instead He said, "It is finished" (John 19:30 ICB). His mission wasn't for fun or adventure or exploration, though. His mission was to die on the cross and be punished for our sins—so that we wouldn't have to be. Three days after Jesus said, "It is finished," God raised Him to life again. But before He returned to heaven, Jesus gave *us* a mission—a task—to accomplish: go and tell the world about Him. Because He didn't come to save *only* you and me. He came to save everyone who chooses to believe and follow Him. But first they have to hear about Him! That's where we come in. We get to be the ones to tell them. How cool is that? So will you say yes to the mission?

GET READY TO MARVEL!

When Jesus returned to heaven, His work wasn't over. Right this minute, He's praying for you (Hebrews 7:25). When someone prays for you, they *intercede* (in-ter-SEED) for you. That means they ask God to help you. You can do that for others too! In fact, before you talk to someone about Jesus, talk to God about that person first. Ask Him to help that person be ready to hear His truth!

GOD, I WANT TO TELL EVERYONE ABOUT YOU. PLEASE SHOW ME HOW I CAN ACCOMPLISH THE TASK JESUS GAVE TO ME. AMEN.

34

SPACE SPIN-OFFS

The true children of God are those who let God's Spirit lead them.

ROMANS 8:14 ICB

DID YOU KNOW NASA invented the cordless vacuum? Along with memory foam mattresses, cell phone cameras, and wireless headphones! Or at least, they sort of did. As NASA worked to land a person on the Moon and a rover on Mars, they needed to invent lots of things. Like wireless headphones for astronauts to talk to each other, lightweight cameras for taking pictures in space, and cordless drills for collecting rock samples from the Moon—after all, there weren't any electrical outlets they could plug into up there on the Moon! NASA's discoveries led to other companies inventing things like the cordless vacuum and the cell phone camera.

Spin-offs of NASA's inventions soon found their way into our everyday lives. Some—like the cordless vacuum—are cool. Others are lifesaving, like the fire-resistant fabric now used in firefighters' gear. And some are life changing, like the cochlear implants that help the deaf hear.

NASA had no idea where all their discoveries would end up. They just did the next thing that needed to be done to complete their mission—inventing along the way. Following God can be a lot like that. Many times, we don't know exactly where He's leading us. That's what happened with the apostle Paul on many of his missionary journeys. Sometimes God said, "Go here but don't go there." Plans could change in the middle of a trip. But Paul's job was the same as our job is now: trust God, follow Him, and do the next thing that needs to be done. God led Paul exactly where he needed to be. And we can count on Him to lead us where we need to be—closer and closer to Him!

DID YOU KNOW?

NASA technology shows up in everything from coffee pots to carbon monoxide detectors and from tennis rackets to athletic shoes. You use it when you scan your groceries at the store and when you save your pictures in the "cloud." And those invisible braces? They're made from the same stuff used in NASA's missile-tracking devices!

GOD, I DON'T ALWAYS KNOW WHERE WE'RE GOING, BUT I'M SO GLAD I'M TRAVELING WITH YOU. AMEN.

35

A LITTLE PULL

Do not let evil defeat you. Defeat evil by doing good.

WHAT DOES THE MOON have to do with the ocean tides? More than you might think!

The ocean's water levels are always changing. They go up and down. The rise and fall of those water levels is called *tides*. Waters rise to high tide, then fall back to low tide. This cycle happens once or twice a day, depending on where you are in the world.

Where does the Moon come in? It's the Moon's gravity that pulls on the waters and makes them rise. Imagine a line going straight out from the Moon and all the way through the Earth. High tides happen on the parts of the Earth that are along that line, while low tides happen on the other parts of the Earth. As the Moon orbits the Earth, the high tides and low tides also move, following the path of the Moon. The Earth's rotation and the pull of the Sun's gravity affect the tides a little. But the Moon has the most powerful pull.

Have you ever felt pulled? Not by the Moon but by people? They can pull you—or push you—to do what they want you to do. And sometimes they might want you to do something wrong. So what should you do? First, try saying, "No, thanks." Then walk away—and pray for them as you go. If saying no doesn't work, you may need to ask your parents or another grown-up you trust for help. And be sure to surround yourself with good friends who love God and will encourage you to do what's right.

GOD, PLEASE GIVE ME THE COURAGE TO SAY NO TO DOING SOMETHING WRONG AND SAY YES TO DOING SOMETHING GOOD AND RIGHT. AMEN.

DID YOU KNOW?

The *Ever Given*—one of the largest container ships in the world—was traveling through the Suez Canal in Egypt in 2021. Suddenly, high winds started blowing it sideways. Mistakes by the crew and canal workers made matters worse, until . . . the ship got stuck! For six days workers tried tugging it out, digging it out, and making the ship lighter. But those things alone didn't work. Then, the Moon came to the rescue! Or at least the tides, which God created the Moon to make, did. Those high tides added a last bit of lift, and the ship was set free.

36

TRUE TREASURES

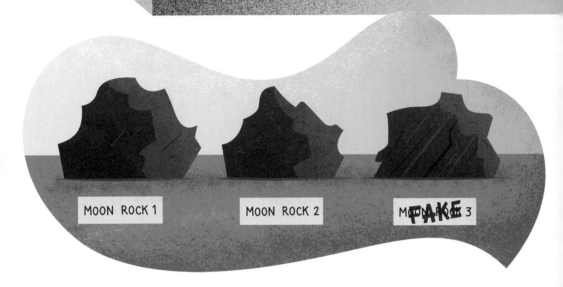

MOON ROCK 1   MOON ROCK 2   MOON ROCK 3 ~~FAKE~~

"Store your treasure in heaven. The treasures in heaven cannot be destroyed by moths or rust. And thieves cannot break in and steal that treasure."

MATTHEW 6:20 ICB

WHEN YOU GO ON a trip, do you collect souvenirs to take home? Maybe some seashells or a cool T-shirt? The astronauts who landed on the Moon picked up a few souvenirs too! Altogether, from the six trips to the Moon, astronauts collected about 842 pounds of rocks. NASA has most of them. Some are still being studied. Others were sent to museums. (You can even touch one if you are ever in Florida at the Kennedy Space Center or at the National Air and Space Museum in Washington, DC.) And some were sent to world leaders as gifts.

Over the years, some of the Moon rocks have been lost, some have been stolen, and some have turned out to be fake! Like the one on display for years in a Dutch museum. Turns out, it wasn't a Moon rock at all. It was just a fossil of wood. No one knows what happened to the real Moon rock. It could have been fake all along!

The treasures of this world—even the treasures of the Moon—don't last. They can be lost or stolen. They can turn out to be worthless and fake. So we don't need to stress over what brand our shoes are or how many birthday gifts we get. Those "treasures" are just *stuff*. If you want to collect real treasures that last forever in heaven, you have to start by giving: give God your love, give help to someone who can't pay you back, and give the good news about Jesus to everyone you can.

DID YOU KNOW?

Like the other missions, Apollo 17 collected rocks and dust from the Moon. Some of those samples were sealed into a special tube while still on the Moon. That tube stayed sealed for almost fifty years. Then, in a *very* slow process that lasted from March 21 until March 22 of 2022, NASA finally opened the tube. The tests and experiments they run will help them get ready for more Moon missions.

LORD, TEACH ME TO COLLECT THE REAL TREASURES THAT LAST FOREVER AND NOT WORRY ABOUT THE TREASURES OF THIS WORLD. AMEN.

37

SO MANY MOONS!

When you are angry, do not sin.

EPHESIANS 4:26 ICB

GUESS HOW MANY MOONS are in our solar system! You'll never guess. Over two hundred! Every planet, except Mercury and Venus, has at least one. Mars has two moons, Neptune has fourteen, Uranus has twenty-seven, and Jupiter has seventy-nine. But Saturn has the most of all: eighty-two! Even little dwarf planet Pluto has five moons of its own. Just a few decades ago, scientists had found only a few moons in our solar system, but now we know there are hundreds. And we keep discovering more and more!

These moons come in all shapes and sizes. The biggest is Jupiter's

Ganymede—it's almost half the size of Earth! Saturn's Hyperion looks like a potato-shaped sponge, while Uranus's Miranda is a mishmash of different landscapes. But Jupiter's Io (EYE-oh) is one of the most interesting. Jupiter's powerful gravity constantly pulls on Io, making its surface rise and fall as much as 330 feet! That's higher than the Statue of Liberty! With hundreds of volcanoes spewing lava miles into the air, Io is *not* somewhere you want to go!

Anger, though, can feel a lot like standing on Io. Emotions can toss us around, and we can be tempted to spew angry words. Some people say, "Just don't get mad." But let's be real. Everyone gets mad. It's what we do with our "mad" that matters.

So don't use anger as an excuse to lose your cool. Step away. Take some deep breaths. Go for a walk. Talk it out with God. And ask yourself if you're angry for a good reason or if you need to let it go. Then, when you're calm, go back and try to make things right again.

DID YOU KNOW?

Jupiter's moon Europa doesn't spew lava—it spews jets of water and ice! Scientists think Europa might have oceans forty to one hundred miles deep that hold about twice as much water as all of Earth's oceans. NASA is sending the Europa Clipper spacecraft there to learn more about this ice-covered moon.

GOD, HELP ME NOT TO GET ANGRY OVER THINGS THAT DON'T REALLY MATTER. AND WHEN I DO GET ANGRY, HELP ME NOT TO LOSE MY COOL AND DO SOMETHING I WILL REGRET. AMEN.

38

FLYING SOLO

Let us think about each other and help each
other to show love and do good deeds.

HEBREWS 10:24 ICB

IMAGINE FLYING AN AIRPLANE. That would be pretty amazing, huh? Now imagine flying that airplane from New York all the way across the Atlantic Ocean to Paris—over 3,600 miles—all by yourself. That would be pretty scary! But that's what a young pilot named Charles Lindbergh did.

You see, years before the world cheered on the Apollo 11 astronauts, people were cheering on Charles Lindbergh. It was May of 1927, and Lindbergh—or "Lucky Lindy"—was about to do what no one had ever done before: fly solo across the Atlantic Ocean. He took off from New York on May 20 in a specially designed plane called the *Spirit of St. Louis*. Thirty-three and a half hours later, he landed in Paris, France. The hardest part of the trip, he said, was staying awake!

Lindbergh didn't fly solo through his whole life, though. Sure, he wanted to reach his own goals, but he also encouraged and helped others succeed too. Like Robert Goddard. Goddard was called the "father of modern rocketry." Lindbergh encouraged him to keep working on his rocket experiments, and those experiments eventually helped launch the Apollo missions into space.

It's great to have goals and go after them. But remember, we don't fly solo through this world. People are all around us, and they need to know that they're not alone. So be the first to say hello to the new kid. Include the people who usually get left out. If someone is struggling with their own goal, encourage them, cheer them on, and help if you can. And most importantly, introduce them to the God who never leaves us to fly on our own!

LORD, PLEASE SHOW ME WHO I CAN ENCOURAGE AND CHEER ON TODAY— AND HELP ME TO DO IT! AMEN.

DID YOU KNOW?

Charles Lindbergh was invited to meet the astronauts of Apollo 8 and watch their launch. When he was told their Saturn V rocket would use twenty tons of fuel per second just to launch them into space, he said, "In the first second of your flight tomorrow, you'll burn ten times more fuel than I did all the way to Paris!"[15]

39

WHERE DOES THE MOON GO?

"The LORD your God goes with you; he will never leave you nor forsake you."

DEUTERONOMY 31:6 NIV

HAVE YOU EVER WONDERED where the Moon goes in the daytime? Nowhere! It's still up there in the sky. And sometimes you can see it. Yes, even when the Sun is shining. And that just feels extra-marvelous!

Conditions have to be just right to see the Moon in the daytime, though. First, the Moon needs to reflect enough of the Sun's light to show up in the blue sky. This usually happens closer to the Full Moon. Also, the Moon must be high enough in the sky to be seen, which means it must be above the horizon (huh-RIE-zuhn)—that's the line that separates the Earth from the sky. That happens for only about twelve hours a day, and only about six of those hours are in the daytime. That's why we can't see the Moon all day long.

The Moon isn't the only "nighttime" object in the daytime sky. All the other planets and stars are up there too—and with the right kind of telescope, you can see them.

Just like God. He's always there. But when problems pop up, when you get tackled by troubles, or when challenges just keep coming, it can be hard to see Him. To help you remember God is always with you, create a memory book. Every time God answers a prayer, helps you, or shows you something amazing about Himself, write it down in a special journal. Add drawings or pictures if you want. And the next time you need a reminder that God is with you, just flip through your book!

GET READY TO MARVEL!

Want to see the Moon in the daytime? It's easiest around the Full Moon. Use a calendar to find out when the next one is—or have a grown-up help you Google it. A few days before the Full Moon, look toward the east just before sunset. And a few days after the Full Moon, look toward the west just after sunrise. (Hint: you'll be looking toward the sky that's opposite the Sun.)

GOD, SOMETIMES I FEEL ALL ALONE, BUT YOU'VE PROMISED TO NEVER LEAVE ME. HELP ME TO SEE THE WAYS YOU ARE WITH ME TODAY. AMEN.

40

JUST ANOTHER TRIP TO THE MOON

This is the day that the Lord has made.
Let us rejoice and be glad today!

PSALM 118:24 ICB

APOLLO 11 ASTRONAUTS LEFT their footprints on the Moon for the very first time in 1969. Just a few months later, Apollo 12 landed two more astronauts on the Moon. So when Apollo 13 headed out for "yet another" mission, taking a stroll on the Moon felt like old news to many Americans. In fact, everything was so routine, NASA's CapCom (the NASA guy who talked to the astronauts) said, "We're bored to tears down here."[16]

Even when the Apollo 13 crew—Jim Lovell, Jack Swigert, and Fred Haise—began broadcasting as they orbited the Moon, not one of the big television stations showed it. As the astronauts toured the ship and showed off their spacesuits, more people were watching the baseball game than them. (Everything changed right after that. Check out page 90!)

Hey, baseball is awesome, but wouldn't you rather watch guys in *actual space*, headed for the *actual Moon*?

In our world, things change fast. Lightning fast. We get so used to looking for newer, bigger, and better that we miss out on the wonders of God's creation. But just look around! From the tiniest bug to the mountains to the Moon, we're surrounded by marvels God has made. All those things aren't there just for us to marvel at. They're there to remind us that God is very real and very much with us (Psalm 19:1; Romans 1:20). Now, that's a reason to be full of joy! And knowing He's with us and ready to help can give us peace and hope on days that aren't so marvelous.

Don't go through this day like it's nothing special. This is the day God made! Be amazed and be glad!

GET READY TO MARVEL!

Here's a mission for you. It's not to the Moon, but it could be just as amazing. With a parent's permission, head outside and look around. Listen. Notice God's creation. If it's daytime, what do you hear? Keep an eye out for the Moon. (Sometimes it can be seen in daytime too.) If it's night, listen for crickets, owls, or coyotes. Check out the stars. Look for the marvelous everywhere you go!

GOD, THANK YOU FOR FILLING THIS WORLD WITH SO MANY MARVELOUS THINGS. HELP ME TO SEE SOMETHING NEW EVERY DAY! AMEN.

41

A SUCCESSFUL FAILURE

> "I have fallen, but I will get up again. I sit in the shadow of trouble now. But the Lord will be a light for me."
>
> **MICAH 7:8 ICB**

HOUSTON, WE'VE HAD A problem." With those five words, everything about the Apollo 13 mission changed.

Apollo 13 was supposed to be the third mission to land men on the Moon. Astronauts James Lovell, Jack Swigert, and Fred Haise were heading for orbit around the Moon. But as they did some routine chores—stirring oxygen and hydrogen tanks—a loud *BANG* echoed through the ship. Warning lights flashed as the astronauts realized things were going really wrong. They were 200,000 miles from home, and the electricity, water, and oxygen systems were all in trouble. Their mission to the Moon quickly became a mission to get home. People around the world watched and prayed.

NASA scientists and engineers worked around the clock. They used math, imagination, creativity, and, of course, duct tape to patch the systems up. *And they did it!* Apollo 13 splashed down in the Pacific Ocean, and the crew was safely picked up by the *USS Iwo Jima* recovery ship.

NASA called Apollo 13 a "successful failure." *Huh? How can a failure be a success?* Well, there's one way—when we learn from it. The things NASA learned made future space missions a whole lot safer.

Sometimes it can feel like you're the only one who messes up. But you're not. Everyone does. Just check out Peter's massive goof. He not only denied Jesus, but he did it three times! Peter was ashamed and scared (Luke 22:54–62), but he was also forgiven by Jesus (John 21:15–19).

Failing isn't the end—whether it's a simple mistake or a great big sin. Failures give us a chance to learn and to ask for God's help and forgiveness. So the next time you mess up and warning lights start flashing in your face, don't give up. Take a deep breath. Ask for forgiveness if you need to. Then get going again. Because *that's* what turns a failure into a success.

LORD, I KNOW I'M GOING TO MESS UP. HELP ME LEARN FROM MY MISTAKES—AND NOT MAKE THE SAME ONES AGAIN! AMEN.

DID YOU KNOW?

After all the problems on Apollo 13, the spacecraft got very cold inside, and water droplets covered the walls, floor, ceiling, and all the instrument panels. As the spacecraft re-entered the Earth's atmosphere, all those droplets caused it to rain inside the spacecraft!

42

HOLES IN THE MOON

Lord, my God, I prayed to you. And you healed me.

PSALM 30:2 ICB

DID YOU KNOW THE Moon is the only planetary body that people have walked on besides the Earth? So what's it like up there? Buzz Aldrin—the second man to walk on the Moon—said the Moon was covered in a dark gray dust. Pebbles, rocks, and boulders were scattered all around.

That's because even though scientists have found traces of water, the Moon is basically a desert covered with plains, mountains, and valleys. And those dark spots you see when the Moon is full? Those are *maria*, which means "seas." But they aren't actually seas. Instead, they're gigantic craters that were filled with lava long ago. Other craters—holes of all shapes and sizes—have been created by countless asteroids (space rocks). They crash into the Moon, tearing up and scarring its surface. Because there's no wind or weather on the Moon, the damage is still there.

Sometimes words can be a lot like asteroids. They can be hard and sharp. They crash into us and create holes in our hearts. It would be easy to take our "craters" and hide away from the world. It'd be easy to avoid making a new friend after an old friend lets us down or to stop trying new things because others laugh when we mess up. But we're not like the Moon. We don't have to hold on to our "craters." Instead, we can tell God all about them (Psalm 62:8), and we can ask Him to help us feel whole again. He'll fill in all the "holes" with His love (Psalm 34:18).

DID YOU KNOW?

Jim Lovell is the only astronaut who visited the Moon twice—on Apollo 8 and Apollo 13—but never got to walk on it. He did get to name part of it, though. As the Apollo 8 navigator, Lovell spotted a small, pyramid-shaped mountain near the Sea of Tranquility. He named it Mount Marilyn in honor of his wife. And astronauts have been using Mount Marilyn to guide them ever since!

LORD, I DON'T WANT THE HURTS OF THE PAST TO KEEP ME FROM LIVING MY BEST LIFE TODAY. PLEASE FILL UP ALL THE HOLES IN MY HEART WITH YOUR LOVE. AMEN.

43

CRUISING ON THE MOON

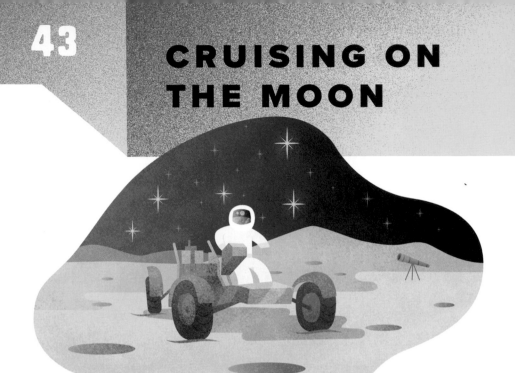

The Lord says, "I will make you wise. I will show you where to go. I will guide you and watch over you."

PSALM 32:8 ICB

THE APOLLO 11, APOLLO 12, and Apollo 14 missions all landed astronauts on the Moon, but those guys were limited to exploring close to their spacecraft. Beginning with Apollo 15, though, the astronauts got wheels! Cars on the Moon? Yep. Officially, they're called Lunar Rover Vehicles, or LRVs. Astronauts use them for EVAs, which is space talk for extravehicular activities.

Apollo 15, 16, and 17 each got their own LRV. The LRVs were folded up and carried to the Moon's surface by the Lunar Module. Once on the Moon, astronauts released the rover, unfolded the wheels, and assembled the frame and seats. An LRV looked like a dune buggy, and it could zip along as fast as eight miles per hour—although the Moon's crater-filled surface made for a bumpy ride!

With each mission, astronauts dared to drive a little farther from their home base camp. Apollo 17 holds the record for the total miles and time driven on a mission at over twenty-two miles in four hours and twenty-six minutes. LRVs allowed NASA to learn so much more about the Moon.

If we want to learn more about God, this world He made, and ourselves, we have to dare to explore too. That might mean stepping out to try a new hobby, sport, or food. It could be traveling to a new city or camping out in the woods—with a grown-up, of course! Whether it's diving into learning something new, reaching out to make new friends, reading through a book of the Bible for the first time, or stepping away for time alone with God, we learn more when we explore. And God is always with us to show us the way!

GOD, WHAT ADVENTURES DO YOU HAVE PLANNED FOR ME TODAY? I WILL TRUST YOU TO SHOW ME WHICH WAY TO GO AND WHAT TO DO. AMEN.

DID YOU KNOW?

When Apollo 17 astronauts Eugene Cernan and Harrison "Jack" Schmitt broke a fender on their lunar rover, there was no repair shop to take it to. So Cernan grabbed some duct tape and patched it right up!

44

SHAKIN' AND QUAKIN'

God did not give us a spirit that makes us afraid. He gave us a spirit of power and love and self-control.

2 TIMOTHY 1:7 ICB

THE MOON IS SHRINKING! And that shrinking is causing *lots* of earthquakes . . . er, um . . . moonquakes. Why is the Moon shrinking? Because its center is slowly, slowly cooling down over time. As it cools and shrinks, the Moon's brittle crust (or outer layer) gets broken up. Some pieces are pushed on top of other pieces. That's called a *thrust fault*. Imagine a balloon with the air slowly leaking out. The more air that leaks out, the smaller and more wrinkled the balloon gets. Then those wrinkles bunch up against each other. That is what's happening on the Moon.

The moonquakes cause landslides on some of the cliff-like formations, and boulders get tossed around. But is any of this something for us to "shake" and "quake" about? No! The Moon is only shrinking about 150 feet every few hundred million years. So no fears here.

There are some things to be afraid of, though. Like wild bears. It's good to have a healthy fear of a mama bear if you're near her cubs in the woods. Other fears—like the fear of trying something new, speaking in public, getting shots, or making new friends—aren't so good. They steal your adventures and shut down your missions to serve God. He didn't create you to live in fear. In fact, when you follow God, He sends His Holy Spirit to live inside you and help you be brave. He might give you a boost of courage just when you need it. He might remind you of a verse that comforts you. Or He might send someone to stand by you. Does that mean you'll never be afraid? No. But it does mean the Holy Spirit will help you do what you need to do—even when you're afraid.

GET READY TO MARVEL!

Is there something you've been wanting to try but you're a little bit scared? Maybe it's trying out for a team or a part in a play. Maybe it's skateboarding, ziplining, or camping out overnight. Talk to God. Talk to your parents. Could it be time to give it a try?

GOD, PLEASE GIVE ME THE WISDOM TO KNOW WHEN MY FEAR IS A HELPFUL KIND OF FEAR—AND WHEN IT'S SOMETHING I SHOULD TRUST YOU TO HELP ME THROUGH. AMEN.

45

WE'LL BE BACK!

**"You should be happy because your
names are written in heaven."**

LUKE 10:20 ICB

APOLLO 11 WAS THE first mission to land men on the Moon, and Apollo 17 was the last. Eugene "Gene" Cernan was one of the astronauts on that last mission to the Moon in 1972. Along with Harrison "Jack" Schmitt, Cernan flew their Lunar Module down to the Sea of Serenity on the Moon's surface. They spent seventy-five hours on the Moon—the longest stay ever (as of 2022). The astronauts did experiments, took thousands of pictures, and collected hundreds of pounds of samples of soil and rock.

Before leaving the Moon, Cernan wrote "TDC" in the Moon's dust—his daughter's initials. Then he gave a quick speech: "We leave as we came, and, God willing, as we shall return, with peace and hope for all mankind."[17] That was over fifty years ago. For so long, it seemed as if we would never return to the Moon—that we had abandoned our explorations. But then—so many years later—we began making plans to go back.

On this Earth, there will be times when you might feel left out, left on your own, or even abandoned by the people around you. But here's some truth you need to remember: when you decide to follow Jesus, your name isn't written in dust—it's written in heaven. Because Jesus *always* wants you with Him. He *never* leaves you on your own. And even though He returned to heaven, He didn't abandon you. His Spirit is with you right now. And He's already made a plan to come back!

GOD, THERE ARE TWO THINGS I CAN KNOW FOR SURE: YOU WILL NEVER LEAVE ME, AND YOU WILL NEVER STOP LOVING ME. AND I'M SO THANKFUL. AMEN.

GET READY TO MARVEL!

Even though we know God is always with us, we can still get lonely sometimes. What can you do when you feel lonely? Ask God to send a friend your way. Ask your parents to help you find a new activity where you can meet new friends. Get up and get moving—go for a walk and spend time praying or singing praise songs to God. Call or text a friend to hang out. Or reach out and help someone. Thinking about God and others will help you not feel so lonely anymore.

46

JUST A HOAX?

While Jesus was praying, heaven opened and the Holy Spirit came down on him. The Spirit was in the form of a dove. Then a voice came from heaven and said, "You are my Son and I love you. I am very pleased with you."

LUKE 3:21–22 ICB

WHEN THE APOLLO MISSIONS landed on the Moon, some people said they never happened. They said the stories were a big hoax—a lie! They believed NASA faked all the Apollo missions, all the launches, all the landings, all the walking around on the Moon—even the astronauts' footprints on the Moon. NASA, they said, made it all up and filmed it like a movie.

And there are some people who still believe that today. Even though the Lunar Reconnaissance (re-CON-neh-zents) Orbiter (OR-bih-ter) has taken pictures of the old Apollo landing sites. Some people see those new pictures and say they're fake too. But perhaps the biggest proof that the Moon landings were real is the fact that the Russians—who were America's biggest competition in the Space Race—also tracked the Moon landings. If they were fake, Russia would have told the whole world so they would still have had a chance to win!

Just like some people say the Moon landings were fake, there are people who say Jesus is not the Son of God. They will tell you that, yes, He lived, but He was just another teacher, just another good man. How can we know Jesus really is God's Son? By what His followers did. They saw Jesus with their own eyes after He rose from the dead, and they couldn't stop talking about Him. They were threatened, beaten, and thrown in prison, but they kept talking about Jesus (Acts 4:19–22). Some even chose to die rather than stop telling people about how Jesus came to save His people!

It's true that people might laugh or look down on you because you say Jesus is God's Son. You might hear someone call Jesus a fake. But you can know the truth. You can know He is the Son of God. He's as real as the footprints on the Moon!

DID YOU KNOW?

There actually was a Moon hoax, but it was all the way back in 1835. A New York newspaper reported that Sir John Herschel looked up at the Moon through his powerful new telescope and saw an entire civilization. There were even unicorns! It was called the Great Moon Hoax, and it was supposed to be a joke—but many people believed it!

GOD, YOU SAID JESUS IS YOUR SON—AND I BELIEVE IT! AMEN.

47

SPINNING AROUND THE SUN

**Do not be interested only in your own life,
but be interested in the lives of others.**

PHILIPPIANS 2:4 ICB

LONG AGO, PEOPLE BELIEVED Earth sat still in space and the Sun, stars, and all the other planets circled around the Earth. But in 1543, Nicolaus Copernicus (nik-uh-lahs koh-PUR-ni-kuhs) publicly shared a different idea: maybe Earth and all the other planets rotated around the Sun. Then, in the 1600s, scientists and astronomers like Galileo Galilei (ga-luh-LAY-oh ga-luh-LAY), Johannes Kepler (yo-HAA-nuhs KEH-plur), and Isaac Newton *proved* that was true—and we've been learning about our solar system ever since.

Our solar system is made up of the Sun, eight planets (Mercury, Venus, Earth, Mars, Jupiter, Saturn, Uranus, and Neptune), dwarf planets like Pluto, hundreds of moons, and millions of asteroids, comets, and meteors. Not only do the planets circle the Sun, but our entire solar system orbits the center of the Milky Way galaxy at a speed of 515,000 miles per hour! (Feeling dizzy yet?)

Just as the other planets in our solar system don't revolve around Earth, other people on Earth don't revolve around us. That means we aren't the center of everyone's world. We don't have to be the center of attention. And we don't have to always have our way.

Sure, it's okay to have wants, hopes, and dreams. Just like it's okay to say what we want for dinner or what movie we want to watch. But we have to remember the world is filled with people who have their own wants too. And they matter to God just as much as ours do. So let's remember that Jesus is the center of everything and try not to make things revolve around us and demand to get our way all the time. Let's let others choose and get their way sometimes too. It's called being "interested in the lives of others," and it's what God asks us to do.

GET READY TO MARVEL!

Want to see what NASA's scientists see in space? Ask a parent to help you take a look for yourself at eyes.nasa.gov. Take a tour around the solar system, check in on the other planets and asteroids, and see what some of the space explorers are up to. You can even see what's happening on Earth!

GOD, PLEASE SHOW ME WHEN I'M TRYING TO BE THE CENTER OF THE WORLD. AND HELP ME TO KEEP JESUS IN MY FOCUS AND THINK ABOUT OTHERS BEFORE I THINK ABOUT MYSELF. AMEN.

48

BUMPING INTO TROUBLE

"I say to you who are listening to me, love your enemies. Do good to those who hate you."

FAR AWAY FROM CITY lights, you can look up on a clear night and see a dusty band of light stretching across the sky. That's the Milky Way galaxy stretching all around us. It's home to our Sun, Moon, Earth, and all the other planets of our solar system—along with about 3,200 other solar systems!

"Milky Way" might sound like a candy bar to us, but it was actually the ancient Romans who came up with the name. Because the dusty band of stars looked like someone had spilled milk across the sky, they called it Via Lactea, which means "milky road" or "milky way."

Scientists believe the Milky Way is about 100,000 light-years across. (Just one light-year is about 5.88 trillion miles.) But our massive Milky Way is about to bump into an even bigger galaxy—the Andromeda Galaxy, which is roughly 220,000 light-years wide! That could be trouble . . . but not for another five billion years or so.

Sometimes we bump into people that we'd rather not. Because, let's be honest, not everyone is nice or a good friend. Some kids cause trouble, and we could get into trouble by hanging out with them. When we love God, though, what do we do about those kinds of kids? First, remember they were made by God, in His image, just like us. We need to love and pray for them. But—and this is really important—it's okay to love and pray for them from a safe distance. You don't have to spend your recess with them, be besties, or invite them to your birthday party. So the next time you bump into someone like that, be kind, smile, say a silent prayer, and keep walking on your way.

DID YOU KNOW?

Romans may have named the Milky Way, but it's the Greeks who helped give astronauts their name. The word *astronaut* comes from two Greek words that mean "space sailor." Anyone who has been launched into orbit or beyond—or who has made "space sailing" their career—can be called an astronaut.

GOD, I'M LEARNING THAT NOT EVERYONE IS A GOOD FRIEND. PLEASE CHANGE THEIR HEARTS AND HELP THEM TO LOVE YOU JUST LIKE YOU HELP ME TO DO. AMEN.

WANT TO BE AN ASTRONAUT?

49

God loves you. And we know that he has chosen you to be his.

1 THESSALONIANS 1:4 ICB

WANT TO BE AN astronaut? NASA is taking applications! There are a few requirements, though. First, you have to be an American citizen. You also need an *advanced* college degree in something like math, computer science, or engineering. Most astronauts are between the ages of twenty-six and forty-six, so you'll need to have a few more birthdays. Oh, and you'll also need to know how to scuba dive. *Wait! Scuba dive?* Yep! Diving deep into the sea helps astronauts practice weightlessness.

If you're accepted, you'll spend two years in training. Then you'll have to pass tests on things like spacewalking, handling robotic equipment, flying a jet, and speaking Russian! For the Artemis missions, which will focus on exploring the Moon's surface and preparing for missions to Mars, only ten people out of over twelve thousand were accepted. More than 11,990 were rejected. And you thought getting a spot on the A team in basketball was tough!

Rejection hurts. And it happens to us all. Maybe you're rejected for astronaut training, the part in the play, or a seat at the table. Or maybe it's when someone says they don't want to be your friend. When rejection happens, you might start to wonder if something is wrong with you. That's when it's time to remember *who* made you: God! And He made you amazing!

Talk to Him about what's going on. Ask Him to help you figure out what to do. You might need to practice and try again. You might need to try something different or new. And you might need to move on and find a different set of friends. Just remember, being rejected isn't the end. It's the beginning of a new part of God's perfect plan.

GOD, YOU KNOW WHAT IT'S LIKE TO BE LAUGHED AT AND REJECTED. IT HURTS. I'M SO THANKFUL I CAN ALWAYS COME TO YOU. AMEN.

DID YOU KNOW?

Even Albert Einstein got rejected! He may have been one of the most brilliant people ever, *but . . .* he flunked his exams in botany (the study of plants), zoology (the study of animals), *and* language. And he couldn't get into school until he passed them. Even then, some of his professors said he'd never graduate. But Einstein kept working—and he later made discoveries in math and science that changed the way we understand the universe!

50

CARRYING THE LOAD

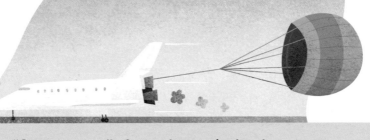

"Come to me, all of you who are tired and have heavy loads. I will give you rest."

MATTHEW 11:28 ICB

IMAGINE A COMBINATION AIRPLANE and rocket that jets you off into space! That's kind of what the Space Shuttle was. It launched into space like a rocket, using boosters to escape Earth's gravity and get into orbit. But when it came time to return to Earth, it landed on a runway like an airplane. The Space Shuttle was the world's first reusable spacecraft. New fuel tanks were needed every time, but the "airplane" part—called the *orbiter*—could be used again and again.

NASA launched five different shuttles into space: the Endeavour, Columbia, Challenger, Discovery, and Atlantis. The first launched in 1981 and the last in 2011. The shuttles flew 135 missions into space. Their cargo compartment was big enough for a school bus to fit inside with room to spare. Their main job was to carry stuff into space. That "stuff" included satellites, space probes, and huge pieces of equipment for building the International

Space Station. One mission even helped repair the Hubble Space Telescope—all while they zoomed around its orbit in space!

Space shuttles may have been built to carry heavy stuff, but you don't have to carry heavy stuff (like problems) on your own. Jesus wants you to let Him do that. But how? It's not like problems come in a box you can just hand over. And while Jesus is always with us, chances are, you can't see Him. So how do you hand over your problem? First, tell Him all about it. (Yeah, He already knows it all. But telling Jesus about the problem helps you hand it over.) Then trust that He's big enough, strong enough, and loves you enough to handle it. That doesn't mean your problem will instantly disappear. But it does mean that Jesus will give you the courage, the wisdom, and the strength to get through it. And it means you can take a rest from stressing about it because you know that you don't have to carry that heavy load all alone.

GOD, NO TROUBLE IS TOO BIG FOR YOU. THANK YOU FOR CARRYING THE HEAVY STUFF FOR ME. AMEN.

GET READY TO MARVEL!

Jesus tells us to love God with all our heart, soul, mind, and strength (Mark 12:30). And while we should love God most of all, this is a great way to love others and help them carry their loads: Love with your *heart* by caring about others. Love with your *soul* by praying for them. Love with your *mind* by thinking about what they're going through and offering ways to help. And love with your *strength* by helping them however you can.

51

"RIDE" IN SPACE

Have courage, and be strong.

1 CORINTHIANS 16:13 ICB

HEADING OUT FOR A ride around the neighborhood is no big deal, right? But when the neighborhood is space? That changes everything! Dr. Sally Ride knew that from experience. Dr. Ride was chosen as one of five astronauts to ride on the Space Shuttle Challenger—a sort of airplane for space (see page 108 for more about the Space Shuttle). It was the first mission for the Challenger, and they launched into space on June 18, 1983.

The astronauts had spent hundreds of hours training for this.

Simulators—like our virtual reality games—showed them how everything would look and sound and feel. But flying inside an actual spacecraft attached to an actual rocket was no game! Sally Ride said that you realize "you're sitting on top of tons of rocket fuel and it's basically exploding underneath you!"[18] Wow! Talk about an exciting—and more than a little terrifying—ride!

Doing something new—whether it's going to space or moving to a new place—can be like that: both exciting and terrifying. If you've ever moved to a new school, started on a new team, or tried a new class, you probably know the feeling. Making new friends in a new place can be tough. It's tempting to hang back and wait for someone to talk to you. Be bold instead. Take the first step. Smile the first smile. Say the first hello. Ask if you can sit with the group. Don't wait for someone to make friends with you. Start out being a friend to them and make the first move! And remember, you're not really on your own—God's right there with you, helping you be brave and bold.

DID YOU KNOW?

When Dr. Mae Jemison flew on the Endeavour on September 12, 1992, she became the first female Black astronaut in space. Jemison was the science mission specialist on the crew. That means she was in charge of scientific experiments on the shuttle. Jemison started her career as a doctor and went on to work with the Peace Corps. Then in 1985, she decided to follow her dream—and became an astronaut!

GOD, WHEN I'M IN A NEW PLACE, PLEASE GIVE ME THE COURAGE TO MAKE NEW FRIENDS—AND TO MAKE THE FIRST MOVE. AMEN.

52

WHAT IS SPACE MADE OF?

We aren't trying to please people. We want to please God.

1 THESSALONIANS 2:4 NIRV

HAVE YOU EVER WONDERED what space is made of? Most everything here on Earth is made up of *matter*—which is anything that takes up space, like dirt, water, air, and even people like us. On Earth, almost all matter is either a solid, liquid, or gas. But in space? Well, that's a whole different matter. (Get it?)

In space, there's a whole lot of a fourth kind of matter called *plasma* (PLAZ-muh). In fact, scientists believe 99.9 percent of the universe is made up of plasma. It acts kind of like a gas, but it also conducts heat and electricity. And when plasma touches a magnetic field, that's when things get interesting!

Plasma can "capture" the magnetic field and fold it into loops. Around the Sun, it can cause sunspots and flares. Here on Earth, you can see plasma at work in fire, fluorescent lightbulbs, and neon lights.

Plasma is created by adding heat or energy to a gas. When the "heat" of pressure is added to our lives, it can change us too. We might feel pressured to play a sport when we'd really rather read a book—or vice versa. We might feel pressured to make our body or our hair look a certain way. Or we might feel pressured to be perfect all the time. These pressures can come from teachers, family, friends, or even ourselves. Most pressures happen because we're trying to please someone else. What we really should be trying to do is please God, and then all those other things will take care of themselves. How can we please God? Look it up in Matthew 22:37–39. When you do those things, it takes the pressure off!

GOD, SOMETIMES THE PRESSURE TO BE PERFECT CAN GET PRETTY HOT. HELP ME TO KEEP MY COOL AND REMEMBER THAT I DON'T HAVE TO BE PERFECT. AMEN.

DID YOU KNOW?

In certain parts of the world—like Alaska, Greenland, Antarctica, and even Montana sometimes—colorful lights dance across the night skies. These are called the *aurora borealis* (uh-RAWR-uh bohr-ee-AL-is). Scientists have discovered that plasma creates these beautiful, shimmering lights. The plasma reacts with the Earth's magnetic fields, creating the billions of tiny flashes of light that make up the ever-changing and swirling lights.

53

NOT-SO-PERFECTLY ROUND

You will teach me God's way to live. Being with you will fill me with joy.

PSALM 16:11 ICB

DO YOU KNOW WHAT would happen if you bounced the Moon like a ball? It would take off in crazy directions! That's because the Moon isn't perfectly round. It's shaped more like an egg. A gigantic, gray, floating-in-space, and circling-around-the-Earth egg.

NASA scientists call that shape an *oblate spheroid* (OB-layt SFEER-oid), which means that instead of being perfectly round, the Moon is slightly flattened at its poles. How does NASA know? The Lunar Reconnaissance Orbiter has been busy taking pictures all around the Moon. Scientists used those pictures and information from other space missions to figure out the Moon's

actual shape. So why does the Full Moon look perfectly round when we see it in the sky? Because we're only seeing part of it.

When we see only part of something, it's easy to think the whole thing is perfect. That's what social media does. It shows us part of someone's life—usually the best parts. We look at those "practically perfect" parts and think their whole life must be like that. We might think, *Wow! He's having amazing adventures. She's got such fabulous friends. Why can't I be more like them?* But remember, people are posting only what they want you to see. They're not showing the not-so-great stuff. Practically nobody shows a picture of that time they struck out, face-planted on the sidewalk, or got a D on their science project.

No, your life isn't perfect—nobody's is. But it can still be wonderful! Stop sitting by yourself and scrolling through other people's lives. Get up and get out and live your own. Follow God, and He'll take you on more adventures than you could ever imagine!

GET READY TO MARVEL!

Take a closer look at the Moon with some binoculars. If the Moon is in the crescent phase, look for the outline of the whole Moon. If it's closer to full, look for the dark patches—they're craters. It's safe to look at a Full Moon with binoculars. But if it's too bright, look for it just as it comes up at dusk. That's called a *moonrise*!

GOD, HELP ME REMEMBER THAT YOU BLESS ME WITH A RICH, FULL, MARVELOUS LIFE EACH AND EVERY DAY! AMEN.

54

OUT OF THIS WORLD

For this world is not our home; we are looking forward to our everlasting home in heaven.

HEBREWS 13:14 TLB

HOW WOULD YOU LIKE to have a sleepover in space—for six months? Astronauts aboard the International Space Station—or ISS—do exactly that!

The International Space Station is sort of like a home, laboratory, and spacecraft all rolled into one. About the size of a football field, the ISS orbits 248 miles above the Earth, zooming through space at 17,500 miles per hour. It circles the Earth once every ninety minutes, so astronauts on board see the Sun rise and set sixteen times every twenty-four hours!

During the astronauts' six-month stay, they stay busy with experiments, taking care of the space station, and spacewalks. Christian astronauts will even watch church online from space! Even though it's pretty amazing to stroll through space, astronauts can get homesick. After spending almost a year in space, astronaut Christina Koch said she missed things like hearing the ocean near her home, feeling wind and rain, and even taking a shower! Space was really cool, but it wasn't really home.

The thing is, Earth isn't really *our* home. That's because we were made to live with God. He's our "home"—not this planet. When we decide to follow God and become part of His family, we can feel like a stranger in this world (1 Peter 2:11). People all around us do wrong things and tell us they're right! It's crazy! And it can make us homesick for heaven. So if you're feeling like an alien in this world, keep doing what's good and right. And remember, Jesus already has a home in heaven ready for you. Just check out John 14:1–3 to find what Jesus said about it!

DID YOU KNOW?

Here's a joke. How do you tie your shoes on the International Space Station? With an astro-knot! Seriously, though, astronauts don't really need shoes in the weightlessness of the ISS. They often wear slipper socks—socks with a soft, leather-like sole on the bottom—to keep their feet warm.

LORD, THANK YOU FOR MAKING A HOME FOR ME IN HEAVEN. AND THANK YOU, JESUS, FOR MAKING A WAY FOR ME TO GET THERE. AMEN.

55

UP CLOSE AND IN YOUR FACE

I look up to the hills. But where does my help come from? My help comes from the Lord. He made heaven and earth.

PSALM 121:1–2 ICB

WHAT HAPPENS WHEN YOU hold your hand up in front of your face? It looks huge, right? But is it really any bigger than when you stretch out your arm and hold your hand away? No. It just looks super-big because it's super-close. The same kind of thing happens with supermoons. A supermoon is when the Moon looks extra-big and bright.

Supermoons happen because the Moon's orbit around the Earth isn't a perfect circle. It's more like an oval, so the distance between the Earth and the Moon changes. When the Moon is closest to the Earth, it's about 226,000 miles away. That's called the *perigee* (PARE-ih-jee). When the Moon is farthest from the Earth, it's about 251,000 miles away. That's called the *apogee* (AP-uh-jee). When a Full Moon happens during the perigee, it's called a *supermoon*.

A supermoon looks 17 percent bigger and 30 percent brighter than a Full Moon at the apogee, when it's farthest away. Supermoons happen only three or four times a year. If you're lucky enough to see one, remember the supermoon isn't really any bigger. It's just closer.

Problems can be like supermoons. That's because when a problem is "up close and in your face," it can look huge! Like a *super-problem*. You might even wonder if God could handle a problem that big. But remember, that problem looks bigger than it really is because it's so close. It's at the top of your mind, and it's hard to see anything else. Stop looking at the problem and look at God instead. As you talk to Him, that problem will shrink back down to a more normal size. And God will remind you that no problem is too big or too tough for Him.

GOD, WHEN MY PROBLEMS LOOK TOO HUGE TO HANDLE, REMIND ME TO STOP LOOKING AT THEM AND LOOK AT YOU. AMEN.

DID YOU KNOW?

Bear. Sturgeon. Beaver. Crow. Those aren't just animals. They're names for Full Moons that happen at different times of the year. Many were named by Native Americans because of what was happening at that time of the year. For example, February has the Bear Moon because that's when bear cubs are born, and March has the Crow Moon because that's when crows return home after migrating for the winter.

56

SHOW 'EM HOW IT'S DONE

You are young, but do not let anyone treat you as if you were not important. Be an example to show the believers how they should live.

1 TIMOTHY 4:12 ICB

CAN'T HANDLE G-FORCES OR small spaces? Don't like flying? There are plenty of reasons why someone can't be an astronaut. But the color of their skin isn't one of them. Yet, when the space program was beginning in the 1950s and 1960s, it was tough for minorities to find a job at NASA.

But in 1983, Guion Bluford became the first African American astronaut as he rocketed off on the Space Shuttle Challenger. That was just the first of four shuttle missions. Altogether, Bluford spend over 688 hours in space. When asked about his astronaut career, Bluford said, "I . . . felt very privileged to have been a role model for many youngsters, including African American kids, who aspire to be scientists, engineers, and astronauts in this country."[19] Bluford knew others were looking up to him, and he decided to be the best example he could be.

Did you know others are looking up to you too? And you can inspire them! How? "Show them with your words, with the way you live, with your love, with your faith, and with your pure life" (1 Timothy 4:12 ICB). Choose to be kind, especially when others aren't. Like when other kids are ignoring the boy who just tripped and spilled his backpack everywhere. Don't ignore him too—lend a helping hand. Stick up for those who can't stick up for themselves, like those who are younger than you. Do what's right even when no one else is. Just because everyone else is cheating doesn't mean you should. And even though it might be awkward at first, talk about God. Let others know you love Him. Don't pray just to be seen but be seen praying and reading His Word. In other words, show 'em how it's done.

GET READY TO MARVEL!

Because you're a kid, you think and talk like a kid. That means you can help other kids in ways grown-ups can't. You can explain the math problem, show them how to do that cool skateboarding trick, invite lonely people to sit with you, and tell them how awesome God is in ways they'll understand. So look around. Who can you help today?

GOD, YOU SENT JESUS TO SAVE ME AND BE MY ROLE MODEL. HELP ME TO BE MORE LIKE HIM SO THAT I CAN BE A GOOD EXAMPLE TO THOSE AROUND ME. AMEN.

57

OUT OF THIS WORLD WORKOUT

Be strong in the Lord and in his great power.

EPHESIANS 6:10 ICB

HOW HARD COULD IT be to float around weightless? Actually, it's harder than you might think—harder on an astronaut's body, that is. Because there isn't gravity in space, the heart and muscles don't have to work as hard, and bones don't have to be as tough. That means they can quickly get weaker. Also, liquid doesn't act the same way in space. Without gravity to pull it down, it sort of "floats" in the body. And since our bodies are about 60 percent water, things change—like the shape of the face and even the shape of the brain!

An astronaut's body ages ten times faster in space, so scientists are searching for ways to make space travel safer. Exercise is hugely important. Astronauts work out about two hours every day. Since they can't go for a swim or jog around the park, NASA had to get creative. There's a "standing" exercise bike with a seatbelt and pedals—but no wheels. Special equipment allows astronauts to lift weights. And a treadmill with bungee cord straps keeps runners from floating away.

Just as astronauts exercise to keep their bodies strong, we need to exercise to keep our faith muscles strong. Without exercise, those muscles get weaker. And a weaker faith makes it easier to slip up and choose to sin. So *dive* into the Bible and read a little every day. *Squat* down on your knees and *lift* up your prayers morning and night. *Warm up* your vocal cords and sing some praises to God. *Run* away from things you know are wrong. *Stretch* out of your comfort zone by talking to others about God. And remember, your greatest strength comes from Him!

DID YOU KNOW?

Astronaut Sunita Williams ran the 26.2-mile Boston Marathon while on board the International Space Station. She ran on a special treadmill and finished in four hours, twenty-three minutes, and ten seconds. Suni ran as fast as eight miles per hour—all while flying through space at more than five miles per second. She even circled the Earth twice as she ran!

GOD, PLEASE REMIND ME TO EXERCISE MY FAITH EVERY DAY. I WANT TO GROW STRONGER AND CLOSER TO YOU. AMEN.

58

THE MOST AMAZING PART

I can do all things through Christ because he gives me strength.

WHAT'S THE TOUGHEST THING about working in outer space? According to astronaut Peggy Whitson, it's the spacewalks—and she should know. Whitson has done ten spacewalks—for a total of sixty hours and twenty-one minutes "walking" around in space. (Seriously, how *cool* is that?)

What makes spacewalks so tough? A lot of it is the suit. Astronauts wear a special spacesuit to protect them and allow them to breathe in space. It's stiff, bulky, and heavy. Moving around in it is like trying to move in a stiff, heavy balloon. One astronaut compared it to a rusty suit of armor—like something a knight from centuries ago would wear. It's tough on the muscles.

Plus, spacewalks often last for hours—with no food! Suits can malfunction, get hit by space junk, or break free from their tether (the line that attaches them to the spacecraft) and drift off into space. But in spite of the danger, Whitson said, "Walking in space is absolutely the most exhilarating part of a mission."[20] In other words, *it's stinkin' awesome!*

So let's get this straight: Spacewalks are the hardest *and* most amazing part of a mission? How's that possible? Because the best things are often found on the other side of hard work. Not everyone wants to do the hard work. And not everyone has the courage to face hard things. That's true on Earth, in space, and for our faith. Jesus asks us to do some hard stuff, like love our enemies, pray for people we don't like, and do the right thing even when it's not cool or popular. But on the other side of those hard things, we find God's peace and joy. And that's the out-of-this-world best part!

DID YOU KNOW?

As of 2022, Peggy Whitson holds the record for most days in space by any American astronaut at 665 days. Most of that time was spent on the International Space Station (ISS). But her record might change. Whitson is planning a trip back to the ISS as commander of a private mission with Axiom Space. She'll add another ten days—or more—to her record!

GOD, HELP ME TO HAVE THE COURAGE TO DO THE HARD THINGS. I WANT TO FEEL THE BEST PARTS OF LIFE—LIKE YOUR PEACE AND JOY! AMEN.

59

"LAUNCH" TIME!

Jesus said, "I am the bread that gives life. He who comes to me will never be hungry. He who believes in me will never be thirsty."

JOHN 6:35 ICB

WHAT'S AN ASTRONAUT'S FAVORITE *time to eat? Launch time!* Seriously, though, what do astronauts eat in space?

The first man in space, Russian Yuri Gagarin, chowed down on beef and liver paste that he squeezed from a tube. *Eww!* At least there was a tube of chocolate for dessert. John Glenn, the first American to eat in space, had a meal of mashed-up beef and vegetables, along with applesauce—all squished into tubes like toothpaste.

Today's astronauts have much better options. A lot of their food is freeze-dried in plastic pouches. This keeps bacteria from growing in it. Astronauts simply add hot water to make it "eat-able." Menus include things like ice cream, macaroni and cheese, and hamburgers, though the buns are replaced with tortillas to avoid crumbs floating around in space. On the International Space Station, astronauts are even learning to grow fresh food, like lettuce.

No matter how inventive NASA's chefs get with space food, no matter how delicious they make it, the astronauts who eat it will still get hungry again. Because food doesn't last. It only fills up our stomachs. It doesn't fill up our hearts and souls. Only Jesus can do that.

Some people try to fill their hearts and souls with other things—like popularity or money. Others stuff their lives with sports, entertainment, or videos on the internet. None of those things last. But Jesus does. When we fill our lives with Him, He fills our hearts and souls with the things that last forever, like His love and joy and peace. And we'll never be empty again.

GOD, FORGIVE ME WHEN I TRY TO FILL UP MY HEART WITH STUFF THAT DOESN'T LAST. PLEASE FILL ME UP WITH YOUR LOVE INSTEAD. AMEN.

DID YOU KNOW?

Taste buds don't work quite the same in space. So astronauts often crave spicy foods—even foods they couldn't eat on Earth. Scientists think it's because zero gravity causes stuffy noses. (Without gravity, noses don't drain.) And since about 80 percent of our taste comes from smells, astronauts don't "taste" the spiciness as strongly as they did on Earth. And the spiciness helps "unstuff" the astronauts' stuffy noses!

60

WHO ATE THE SUN?

**Lord, you give light to my lamp. My God
brightens the darkness around me.**

PSALM 18:28 ICB

THE SUN HAS BEEN *eaten.* At least that's what ancient Chinese scribes wrote in roughly 1200 BC. What on Earth were they talking about? Nothing on Earth actually. They were talking about something that happened in space when the Moon, Earth, and Sun all lined up just right. That something was a *solar eclipse* (SOH-ler ih-KLIPS)—although they didn't know that then.

In a solar eclipse, the Moon moves between the Sun and Earth, blocking out the Sun's light. The Moon might block part of the Sun, which is called a *partial eclipse.* Or it might block all of it—a *total eclipse.* Which explains how those ancient people thought the Sun had been eaten!

Solar eclipses happen about four to seven times a year. They make the world a little darker than it usually is. Kind of like tough times. Troubles can block the light of our happiness and make everything seem darker. But no matter how dark or sad things might be, God is still lighting up this world with His goodness. He's still listening to prayers and answering them. He's still forgiving and loving. He's still helping His people to love like He does.

So when your world seems dark with troubles, look for His light. Look for the good things happening around you. Like people being kind to each other, helping those who can't help themselves, or even taking care of our world by picking up trash. Look for the things that make you smile, like watching puppies chasing their tails or getting hugs from someone who loves you. And most of all, look *to* God. Ask Him to chase away the darkness and show you the light of His goodness.

GET READY TO MARVEL!

When your world feels dark, it's okay to feel sad. It's also okay to let some "light" and happiness in. Dance to a happy song. Watch a funny movie. Take a walk. With a parent's help, find out when the next eclipse is going to be and make plans to view it. Or find a comfy spot and talk to God. Ask Him to remind you of how much He loves you.

GOD, WHEN I'M HAVING A TOUGH TIME, HELP ME TO SEE YOUR GOODNESS ALL AROUND ME. AMEN.

You are all around me—in front and in back.
You have put your hand on me.

PSALM 139:5 ICB

SPACE FORCE—IT'S NOT JUST for science fiction and movies anymore. It's for real! In 2019, the United States Space Force—or USSF—joined the Army, Navy, Air Force, and Marine Corps as the newest branch of America's armed forces that support the space mission. Instead of soldiers, Space Force has guardians. And they're on a mission to guard our space.

Space itself doesn't belong to any one country, but we have lots of satellites

that need protecting from our enemies. Those satellites are important because our lives are filled with technology—like the GPS that gets us to Grandma's house, the cell phones we use to call friends, and the internet we surf. Even things like banking, 911 calls, and our nation's electricity tap into the power of satellites. Space Force even tracks all the space junk to make sure it doesn't hit a satellite or the International Space Station! Their motto is *semper supra*, which means "Always Above," because Space Force is always watching what happens above.

Semper supra would be a pretty good motto for God too. He's always above, watching over us. He's ready to protect us from our enemy, Satan, who is always on the prowl and just waiting to pounce (1 Peter 5:8). But God keeps track of him. He always knows where the enemy is and what he's up to, so He's ready to defend us from any attack. He's not only always above us, but He's also beside us, before us, behind us, *and* with us. God protects us whenever and wherever we go!

DID YOU KNOW?

The Space Force logo is more than a cool symbol. Every part means something special. The outer edge represents protection from all enemies. The inner two spires—or points—are for rockets launching into space. The black coloring inside is for the darkness of space. And the star is Polaris—or the North Star—which is often used for guiding sailors. Even space sailors!

GOD, YOU ARE AMAZING! YOU KNOW EVERYTHING, SEE EVERYTHING, AND CAN DO ANYTHING. I KNOW I'M SAFE AND SECURE WITH YOU. AMEN.

62

A SAFE LANDING

**He is my place of safety and my Savior. He
is my shield and my protection.**

PSALM 144:2 ICB

WOULD YOU DARE TO go farther into space than any human
has ever gone? That's what the astronauts of future Artemis missions hope to do. And they'll do it using the Orion spacecraft. It's
NASA's newest spacecraft, and it will hold everything the astronauts need to
live and work for up to twenty-one days.

Orion's main tasks will be to carry astronauts safely into space, be their home and office while in space, and bring them safely back to Earth when their mission is complete. But Orion also has one more job: to be the "lifeboat" if something goes wrong during the launch. In an emergency, the Orion will activate the Launch Abort System. In just milliseconds—way less than a single second—it will push the Orion and its crew away from the Space Launch System, helping the crew land safely.

Getting pushed away from an out-of-control rocket is a good thing. But do you know what's not so good? Being pushed away from others. So what should we do when we're left out, made fun of, or ignored? First, admit that it hurts—because it does. Then, decide not to hurt back (Matthew 5:38–40). Instead, look around for others who've been pushed away too. Chances are, you're not the only one, and you might find that those kids are some of the best friends you'll ever have. In the meantime, talk to God and spend some time in His Word. He's always your safe place to land.

GOD, THANK YOU FOR ALWAYS BEING THE ONE I CAN RUN TO. I KNOW I AM SAFE WITH YOU. AMEN.

DID YOU KNOW?

A gigantic shiny gumdrop! That's what the crew module of the Orion spacecraft is shaped like. Four astronauts will live and work inside that "gumdrop." It has a living space of only about 316 cubic feet. How big is that? Think about how big your bedroom is. About four of these modules would fit in there! Inside that tiny space, NASA has carefully crammed everything the astronauts will need to work, eat, sleep, and exercise for weeks. Amazing!

63

SUPER GUPPY TO THE RESCUE!

Each of you received a spiritual gift. God has shown you his grace in giving you different gifts. And you are like servants who are responsible for using God's gifts. So be good servants and use your gifts to serve each other.

1 PETER 4:10 ICB

WHEN YOU'VE GOT A name like Super Guppy—and a shape to match—it's hard to look tough. But Super Guppy does a tough job, and it does it with its nose! The nose of this unusual aircraft actually opens up to reveal a super-huge cargo area. It's 25 feet wide and 111 feet long and one of the largest cargo areas of any plane. Super Guppy is basically a big plane that can carry a small plane inside.

Super Guppy carries rocket and spacecraft parts that are too big for trucks and trains to carry across land. And it does it much faster than boats and barges could. The first, slightly smaller Guppy—called the Pregnant Guppy—was built in 1961 and delivered parts for the early Apollo missions. An even bigger Super Guppy was built in 1965 and flew over three million miles for NASA missions. The latest Super Guppy Turbine delivered parts for the Artemis missions.

Super Guppy was specially built to do what NASA wanted it to do. And you were specially "built" by God to do what He wants you to do. To help you accomplish your mission, God gave you a special gift. That *gift* is something you're extra-good at doing. It could be teaching, being generous, or sharing your faith. It might be having faith, helping, or encouraging. Your gift might change as you grow up. Whatever your gift is, God wants you to use it to share His love and the truth about Jesus with everyone you can!

GET READY TO MARVEL!

Gather up your friends— and try to include someone new. Talk about the gifts God has given each of you. (Sometimes others can help you see what you're extra-good at.) Brainstorm ways to use your gifts to tell others about God, like teaching a Bible story to younger kids. Offer to pray with people or volunteer to help a charity. Be creative! What can you do?

GOD, SHOW ME THE GIFT YOU'VE GIVEN TO ME—AND HOW TO USE IT TO TELL OTHERS ABOUT YOU. AMEN.

64

RIDING ON A ROCKET

God's power is very great for us who believe. That power
is the same as the great strength God used to raise Christ
from death and put him at his right side in heaven.

EPHESIANS 1:19–20 ICB

SPACECRAFTS DON'T JUST FLY off into space— they need
to ride on a rocket to get there! When the Apollo 11 mission headed
for the Moon in 1969, the spacecraft rode on the Saturn V rocket.
The Saturn V stood 363 feet tall, or about as tall as a thirty-six-story building.
It had 7.5 million pounds of *thrust*. (That's the force pushing down against the
Earth.) That's 160 million horsepower! Saturn V was so powerful that it could
launch four school buses to the Moon—or one command module, one lunar
module, and three astronauts.

But the rocket that sent the Artemis I mission to the Moon is even more powerful. It's called the Space Launch System (SLS). Nicknamed the Mega Moon Rocket, it's the most powerful rocket ever built! At 322 feet tall, it's a little shorter than the Saturn V, but it has 8.8 million pounds of thrust. It pushed Artemis's Orion spacecraft at a speed of 24,500 miles per hour!

That kind of power is amazing, but it's nothing compared to the power of God. Not just the power to create oceans, mountains, and animals of every kind. God even has the power to raise the dead to life again—like when He raised Jesus from the dead. But God's power doesn't stop there! When He raised up Jesus, He also knocked down sin and death. Because of God's great power and love, sin can't separate us from Him anymore. And death is gone because we can live with Him forever. All we have to do is believe that Jesus is God's Son and then love and follow Him. Now that's some awesome power!

DID YOU KNOW?

The SLS rocket needs an enormous amount of fuel just to get off the ground and pull away from Earth's gravity. Its two booster rockets burn six tons of solid fuel *every second* for about two minutes! And its four engines use a fuel made of liquid hydrogen and liquid oxygen. They'll burn for about eight minutes, burning up ninety thousand gallons *every minute!*

GOD, YOUR POWER IS MARVELOUS AND AMAZING! THANK YOU FOR USING YOUR POWER TO SAVE ME FROM SIN. AMEN.

65

WORTH THE WAIT

Dear friends, now we are children of God. We have not yet
been shown what we will be in the future. But we know
that when Christ comes again, we will be like him.

1 JOHN 3:2 ICB

ROCKETS TRAVEL THOUSANDS OF miles per hour, but not
every machine NASA builds moves super-fast. Some of them move
super-slow. Like the Crawler. Its name matches its speed, but the
Crawler does a super-important job that no other machine can do.

Crawler is short for Crawler-Transporter. NASA has two of these huge
machines: Crawler-Transporter 1 and Crawler-Transporter 2. Not the best names,
right? Their nicknames are cool, though: Hans and Franz. Each machine is about
the size of a baseball diamond (the part of a baseball field inside the bases).

The Crawlers were built in 1965 to move the gigantic Saturn V rocket
from the assembly building to the launchpad. When carrying a rocket, these
mechanical beasts move at a lightning-fast 1 mile per hour—and the driver still

wears a seatbelt! (You probably walk about 2.5 miles per hour, so this would be your only shot at zooming past a rocket ship!) The Crawlers, which look like gigantic tanks, do the heavy lifting for NASA rocket launches. They don't move fast, but when you need to move a rocket, it's worth the wait!

Like those Crawlers, time can feel like it's crawling by. Maybe it's when the school day drags on, and you think the clock will *never* say it's time for recess, lunch, or the end of the day. Or maybe it's Christmas, your birthday, or a big vacation that seems like it'll never come. When time is ticking by slower than a turtle waking up from a nap, waiting can be *really* frustrating. Or . . . it could be fun. *How?* By thinking about how great it'll be when it's finally time for recess, your birthday, or that big vacation.

There's one thing the whole universe is waiting on—for Jesus to come back! We don't know when that will be or how long we'll have to wait, but just think how wonderful that day will be. Jesus is definitely worth the wait!

DID YOU KNOW?

Crawler-Transporter 2 is over fifty years old, so NASA recently treated it to a makeover. They gave this hefty machine the extra strength it needed to move the massive Space Launch System (SLS) rockets for the Artemis missions to the Moon. These SLS rockets are the most powerful ever launched— even stronger than the mighty Saturn V that took Buzz Aldrin and his communion to the Moon (see page 64)!

GOD, HELP ME NOT TO THINK ABOUT THE WAITING SO I CAN THINK ABOUT HOW WONDERFUL IT WILL BE WHEN JESUS COMES BACK. AMEN.

66

GO OR NO GO?

What if someone is caught in a sin? Then you who live by the Spirit should correct that person. Do it in a gentle way.

GALATIANS 6:1 NIRV

GO OR NO GO? That's the question NASA engineers and scientists ask about each of the systems needed for a space mission. *Go* means everything is ready to go, and *no go* means something isn't working right. A no go for a system might cause NASA to say, "Abort!" What does that mean? *Abort* means "the unscheduled termination of a mission prior to its completion."[21] *Umm, what?* In other words, it means stopping a mission before it's finished.

NASA can abort a mission before the rocket ever leaves the ground. That's what happened in 2022, when a fuel leak stopped the Artemis I launch. Other

times, the spacecraft might be far away from Earth. Like in 1970, when an explosion on Apollo 13 meant the astronauts had to abort their mission to land on the Moon. NASA's mission then changed to getting the astronauts home safely (which they did; see page 90 to learn more about it).

NASA isn't the only one who needs to stop a mission now and then. Sometimes we need to call out "no go" too. It can even happen in our friendships. That might mean standing up to a friend and telling them to stop picking on another kid. It might mean telling them to stop talking behind another friend's back. Or it might mean telling them to stop using bad words. If a friend won't stop doing that thing that is hurtful, wrong, or even dangerous, you might have to stop being friends for a while. If that happens, be as kind as you can. Remember that you make mistakes too. Keep praying for them, and maybe one day you'll be able to be friends again.

GOD, GIVE ME THE COURAGE TO TELL MY FRIENDS WHEN THEY'RE DOING THINGS THAT ARE WRONG—AND HELP ME TO BE KIND AND GENTLE WHEN I DO. AMEN.

DID YOU KNOW?

What's the number one reason for aborted missions? Weather! Launches typically happen in Florida where storms and even hurricanes are frequent. Lightning is especially dangerous because it can zap the electronics that tell the spacecraft where to go. In 1969, Apollo 12 was hit by lightning twice as it flew up through the clouds! So NASA now keeps an extra-close eye on the weather.

67

THE BEST IT CAN BE

Jesus said to the followers, "Go everywhere in the world. Tell the Good News to everyone."

MARK 16:15 ICB

WHAT'S A WET DRESS rehearsal? Well, it doesn't mean everyone wears funny clothes and gets soaked with water. A wet dress rehearsal is what NASA did before launching the Artemis I mission into space. They rehearsed—or practiced—as much as they could without actually launching the rocket. First, NASA rolled the Space Launch System rocket and Orion spacecraft onto the launchpad. All the power systems were connected and turned on. Next, more than seven hundred thousand gallons of fuel were loaded into the rocket. (That's why it's called a "wet" dress rehearsal.)

NASA then started the countdown to launch. They practiced talking to all

the different team members. They practiced stopping and restarting the countdown. They even practiced canceling the launch. When it was over, the fuel was drained out, and the spacecraft was rolled back into storage. Why did NASA do all that practicing? Because they wanted the mission to be the best it could possibly be.

Jesus gave you a mission too: to tell others about Him. But that's not something you can just "launch" yourself into. First, you need to get ready. Just as NASA builds its rockets and spacecraft, you need to build your relationship with God by reading and studying His Word. After all, you need to *know* God before you can share Him with others. Next, you need to practice what you're going to say. Kind of like NASA's dress rehearsal but minus the rocket fuel. Start by asking God to guide your words. Then practice them with your parents, with a friend, or in front of a mirror. God will help you figure out what to say (Luke 12:12). The more you practice, the easier it will be—and that will help your mission become the best it can be!

DID YOU KNOW?

The Artemis I mission took the spacecraft 270,000 miles away from Earth. Altogether, the spacecraft traveled over 1.4 million miles in a trip that took twenty-six days! NASA hopes to someday send a mission to Mars. Astronauts would have to travel approximately 140 million miles to the red planet—and then travel back home again.

GOD, I WANT TO TELL MY FRIENDS ABOUT YOU. TEACH ME MORE ABOUT YOU FROM THE BIBLE AND HELP ME KNOW JUST WHAT TO SAY. AMEN.

68

RED CREW TO THE RESCUE

Our love should not be only words and talk. Our love must be true love. And we should show that love by what we do.

1 JOHN 3:18 ICB

TAKEOFF ALMOST DIDN'T HAPPEN. As NASA prepared for Artemis I to launch, they realized there was a leak. This was no ordinary leak either. It was a hydrogen leak. Which meant there was a danger of the whole thing exploding! Would NASA have to cancel the launch? Not this time! That's because the red crew rushed to the rescue. The red crew is a team of NASA experts who wait near the launch site, ready to step in and make any needed repairs. That day, three men—Chad Garrett, Billy Cairns, and Trent Annis—went to the launchpad, checked out the rocket's leak,

pulled out their tools, and fixed it. Their job was extremely dangerous—so dangerous that NASA's Mission Control team stayed *four miles* away from the launch site!

NASA can make some repairs just by punching a few commands into the computer. But there are other times when words aren't enough. They need the red crew to run to the rescue.

There will be a day when a friend needs you to run to the rescue. That's when you'll be put to the test. It will be easy to say, "I'll pray for you" and then go on about your day. It's easier to not get too close to anything uncomfortable or difficult. Of course, praying is absolutely what you should do, but you need to be willing to help too. That might mean studying with a friend for that impossible test, standing up with them when that bus-stop bully comes around, or offering a hug when it feels like their whole world has come tumbling down. Words are wonderful, but when a friend needs help, be ready to do more. Be ready to run to the rescue—and as you run, be sure to ask God to help you.

GOD, PLEASE GIVE ME A HEART THAT'S WILLING TO HELP MY FRIENDS. ESPECIALLY WHEN IT'S NOT EASY. AMEN.

69

SUPER-AMAZING SUPERCOMPUTER

Trust the Lord with all your heart. Don't depend on your own understanding.

PROVERBS 3:5 ICB

C AN YOU BLOW A bubble while doing your math homework? Could you sing a song at the same time? How about answering a question from your mom too? It's hard for us to think about more than one or two things at once. But computers? That's a whole different story.

Like the computer helping put the Artemis missions into space. It is called the *Aitken supercomputer*, and it's NASA's most powerful computer. The Aitken is built in modules—kind of like massive, electronic Legos. NASA can keep adding modules, making the supercomputer more and more powerful. So don't expect this computer to fit in your backpack. Its "brain" is so big, it needs whole buildings!

The Aitken solves big problems super-fast. It can simulate (or act out) a rocket launch and "think" about rocket power, the launcher, the space-craft, and more—*all at the same time!* These simulations make real missions with real astronauts safer by figuring out problems ahead of time.

Faith is a lot like that supercomputer. No matter how awesome it is, you can always add to it and make it even more powerful. You see, faith is knowing that God is real and trusting Him to keep His promises, even though you can't see Him (Hebrews 11:1). When you choose to trust Him and then see Him answer a prayer, like helping you find a new friend, you learn to trust Him even more. And that means your faith is getting bigger, just like the Aitken supercomputer gets bigger when a new module is added. Faith will do something a whole lot more amazing than take you to the Moon, though. It will take you to God, and He'll carry you all the way to heaven.

DID YOU KNOW?

The Aitken supercomputer runs at over 13 petaflops. What's a petaflop? It's a way of measuring a computer's speed. Just one petaflop means that a computer can "think" about a quadrillion (1,000,000,000,000,000) operations per second. One of the world's fastest computers, as of 2022, is Tesla's Dojo, which can run at 1.8 exaflops—it "thinks" about 1.8 quintillion (1,800,000,000,000,000,000) things per second!

GOD, I DO TRUST YOU. TEACH ME TO TRUST YOU EVEN MORE! AMEN.

70

"SNOOPING" AROUND

You are chosen people. You are the King's priests. You are a holy nation. You are a nation that belongs to God alone.

1 PETER 2:9 ICB

AT NASA EVERYTHING HAS a name, and many things have nicknames. Like the Space Launch System rocket that powered the Artemis I to the Moon. Its nickname is Mega Moon Rocket. Much cooler!

Some of the best nicknames, though, were part of the Apollo 10 mission. This mission was going to be like practice for the Moon landing of Apollo 11. Except the Apollo 10 Lunar Module wasn't going to land on the Moon. It was just going to fly close to the surface and "snoop" around for a possible landing site. That "snooping" is why the Apollo 10 Lunar Module was nicknamed Snoopy, after Charles Schulz's cartoon character. So naturally the Command Module was nicknamed Charlie Brown, after Snoopy's cartoon pal. Later, when the Lunar Module returned to the Command Module after its trip down to the Moon, astronaut Thomas Stafford said, "Snoopy and Charlie Brown are hugging each other."[22] Even the caps Apollo astronauts wore under their helmets were called "Snoopy caps" because of their Snoopy-looking ears.

Nicknames like Charlie Brown and Mega Moon Rocket can be fun. But some nicknames aren't so fun. In fact, they can be downright hurtful and hateful. Whether it's the names someone else calls us or the names we sometimes call ourselves, God wants us to remember that our only true names are the ones He gives us.

Do you want to know some of God's nicknames for You? "Snoop" around verses like John 15:15, Matthew 5:13, Matthew 5:14, and 1 John 3:1. What does God call you?

DID YOU KNOW?

Snoopy quickly became a mascot for NASA. In specially drawn comic strips, the cartoon pup even landed on the Moon months *before* the Apollo 11 astronauts. And over fifty years later, a stuffed Snoopy traveled into space as the zero-gravity indicator. That means, when he floated up into the air, Mission Control knew weightlessness had been achieved.

LORD, IT'S EASY TO BELIEVE THE BAD THINGS PEOPLE SAY ABOUT ME. WHEN THAT HAPPENS, HELP ME REMEMBER THAT WHAT YOU SAY IS THE ONLY THING THAT MATTERS. AMEN.

71

MOONIKIN TO THE MOON!

"Do for other people what you want them to do for you."

LUKE 6:31 ICB

MOONIKIN MADE IT TO space! Who's that, you ask? Well, Moonikin isn't a *who*; he's a *what*. Moonikin is a mannequin (MAN-eh-kin). *Get it?* His full name is Commander Moonikin Campos, and he's one of three "astronauts" that orbited the Moon on the Artemis I mission in 2022. Flying along with him were Helga and Zohar. They're called *phantoms* (FAN-tums) because they don't have arms or legs, just a head and body, which is a little creepy.

Why did NASA send mannequins into space? Because one day missions—like Artemis II—will be taking *real* people to the Moon. NASA wanted to be extra-sure the Orion spacecraft and Space Launch System rocket were safe for humans. So Moonikin, Helga, and Zohar were made. Their bodies are made of special materials that act like human bones and tissues. They're loaded with sensors to measure the effects of blastoff and spaceflight on the body. They can also keep track of radiation. Moonikin, Helga, and Zohar might be fake astronauts, but they're a real help to NASA's research.

Fake astronauts might be a good thing, but fake friends definitely are not! Fake friends are the ones who pretend to be your friend but then laugh behind your back. They include you only when they need something, and they don't stick up for you. When times get tough, fake friends are nowhere to be found. What could be worse than finding out a "friend" is being fake? Being a fake friend yourself! Choose to be a true friend instead. How? By treating others the way you would want them to treat you. It's called the Golden Rule, and it will make your friendships shine!

GET READY TO MARVEL!

Want to be a marvelous friend? Here are some tips: Ask questions about the things they're interested in—and listen to the answers. Invite them to hang out with you. Share your thoughts and feelings. Be kind. Remember their birthday. Stick up for them. Help when they need help. Keep your promises. Basically? Be the kind of friend you want others to be to you.

GOD, I DON'T WANT TO BE A FAKE FRIEND. PLEASE HELP ME TO LOVE OTHERS AND BE A TRUE FRIEND TO THEM. AMEN.

72

BACK TO THE MOON

If we confess our sins, he will forgive our sins.

1 JOHN 1:9 ICB

THE LAST TIME A human rocketed around the Moon was in 1972. More than fifty years ago! But NASA's Artemis II mission plans to return humans to the Moon sometime in the 2020s—or at least orbit around it.

The Artemis II mission will use the Space Launch System—also known as the Mega Moon Rocket—to launch the Orion spacecraft with four astronauts on board into space. They'll loop around the Earth twice to pick up speed and then zoom off to orbit the Moon. Astronauts will spend eight to ten days living and working in the Orion spacecraft. Then, they'll tap into Earth's gravity to pull them back for a splashdown in the Pacific Ocean. If Artemis II is a success, those astronauts will have traveled farther into the solar system than any human being has ever been.

Getting back to the Moon is a mission that will take years of work and a few billion dollars. But when you've messed up—when you've sinned—and need to get back to a good relationship with God, that's a mission that can happen in an instant, no matter how badly you've messed up. It doesn't even cost a penny because Jesus already paid for our sins on the cross. You just need to tell God that you know you've done wrong. That's called *confession* (kuhn-FESH-uhn). Next, tell Him how sorry you are and that you'll try to never do that wrong thing again. That's called *repentance* (re-PEN-tense). Confession and repentance bring you right back to God. And the trip won't be far because God will already be running to meet you (just check out Luke 15:20).

GET READY TO MARVEL!

God doesn't stop loving you when you mess up and when you sin. Not even for a second. And when you come back to Him, He doesn't want you to feel guilty or ashamed. Read Luke 15:11–24. What did the father do for the son who came back home? He threw a celebration. And that's just what God, our Father, will do for everyone who comes back to Him (Luke 15:7).

GOD, I KNOW I MESS UP. PLEASE SHOW ME WHEN I DO AND HELP ME TO GET BACK TO YOU AS FAST AS I CAN. AMEN.

In Christ, there is no difference between Jew and Greek. There is no difference between slaves and free men. There is no difference between male and female. You are all the same in Christ Jesus.

GALATIANS 3:28 ICB

WHAT COULD BE BETTER than making history? Making history twice—in just one trip! That's what the Artemis III mission is planning to do.

Artemis III is scheduled to launch sometime in the 2020s. It will be the first mission to land people on the Moon since Apollo 17 in 1972. Four astronauts will travel in the Orion spacecraft and orbit the Moon. Two astronauts will then pilot a lunar lander—SpaceX's new Starship—down to the Moon. They'll spend 6.5 days near the Moon's south pole. That's the longest stay ever! Four moonwalks are planned. (A moonwalk is when astronauts leave their spacecraft to walk around on the Moon. Wearing space-suits, of course.) Their main mission will be searching for water (in the form of ice) under the Moon's surface.

Those two astronauts will make history. That's because one will be a woman—the first woman *ever* to step onto the Moon. And the other will be the first person of color *ever* to walk on the Moon. Why is that important? Because for too long, women and people of color were left out, or worse. But our world is learning that we need to include everyone.

You can help. Remember, Jesus didn't come to save only the people who looked like Him. He doesn't love people only from a certain country. There's room at Jesus' table for everyone who wants to be there. So when you're hanging out with friends, invite others to join you. Pick the one who's always left out to be on your team. And, yeah, make room at the lunch table. Because that's what Jesus would do. And He loves to see you loving like He does!

GET READY TO MARVEL!

There's something about food that makes friendships easier. If you want to learn more about someone's culture, try visiting a restaurant that specializes in that culture's food—or try out a recipe at home. If you have a friend from that culture, invite them along. And maybe share a favorite food from your home too.

GOD, TEACH ME TO SEE EVERYONE AS YOU SEE THEM—SOMEONE YOU LOVE AND SOMEONE YOU WANT ME TO LOVE. AMEN.

74

MINING ON THE MOON

The Spirit gives him wisdom, understanding, guidance and power. And the Spirit teaches him to know and respect the Lord.

ISAIAH 11:2 ICB

MINING ON THE MOON? That's what NASA is planning. They won't be mining for silver or gold, though. They'll be mining for ice and water. And when you're in the desert of space—where water is super-rare—that's far more valuable than jewels!

The information gathered by the Lunar Reconnaissance Orbiter and the Lunar Crater Observation and Sensing Satellite has helped scientists in their search for water on the Moon. They've discovered enough frozen water to fill twenty-four gallon jugs. That might not sound like much, but NASA is convinced they'll find even more.

Why is water so important? Not only is it needed for people to work on the Moon, but it can also be split into hydrogen and oxygen to make rocket fuel. Being able to fuel a spacecraft on the Moon would make travel into deeper space much easier. The Moon's water could turn it into a sort of "gas station" to help travelers fill up for a mission to Mars!

Jesus offers us an even more powerful kind of water, though. It won't take us to another planet, but it will power us through life on this world and all the way to heaven with Him. It's not the kind of water we drink. And it's not really an "it"—it's a He. He's the Holy Spirit of God. Jesus calls Him the Living Water because He's alive and because He quenches our thirst for God and His goodness (John 4:1–14). How can we get this Living Water? By believing in Jesus! When we follow Him, the Holy Spirit of God comes to live inside us and makes a river of life flow out from our hearts. He fills us up with His wisdom, courage, and strength—and fuels us with all the power we'll ever need to keep following Jesus.

DID YOU KNOW?

There is water on the Moon—and it hops! NASA scientists have discovered tiny molecules of water on the Moon's surface. As the Sun warms the surface during the lunar day, the water molecules rise up and float around until they bump into a colder spot. Then, the cold makes them fall back to the surface again!

GOD, PLEASE FILL ME UP WITH THE LIVING WATER OF YOUR HOLY SPIRIT. I NEED HIS HELP TO FUEL ME THROUGH EVERY DAY. AMEN.

75

GATEWAY TO THE MOON— AND MORE!

Give thanks as you enter the gates of his temple.
Give praise as you enter its courtyards. Give
thanks to him and praise his name.

PSALM 100:4 NIRV

IMAGINE A SORT OF "space hotel" that would allow you to zip down to the surface of the Moon pretty much whenever you wanted. That's what NASA scientists are hoping the Gateway project will one day make possible.

Gateway will be a space station that will orbit the Moon. Even though it won't launch right away, pieces of it are being built right now. Gateway will have two main parts: the PPE (Power and Propulsion Element) that will take care of all its energy needs, and the HALO (Habitation [hab-ih-TAY-shuhn] and Logistics [luh-JIS-tiks] Outpost) where astronauts can live and work for up to three months. Gateway will also have spots for visiting astronauts to "park" their space-craft. There's even a way to add on rooms if more people want to come! It could even become like a rest stop and gas station for launching missions deeper into space.

Staying close to the Moon will allow astronauts and scientists to get a better, longer look at it. And trips down to the Moon's surface will be much easier from Gateway than traveling all the way up from Earth!

Just as this space station will be a "gate-way"—a way to get to the Moon—worship is also a gateway. Not to the Moon but to God. When we worship Him, we actually meet with Him, and His presence surrounds us. But maybe you're wondering what worship is exactly. It's simple: it's telling God how amazing He is. Worship also reminds us that we're not alone, He's in control, and we can trust Him. We can worship God with songs, with art, or with words written on a page. Or we can worship by simply thinking about how wonderful, how powerful, and how marvelous He is!

GET READY TO MARVEL!

Tell God how marvelous He is. Draw it in a picture. Sing it in a song. Write it in a poem. Dance out your praise to Him. Shout it, whisper it, or express it using sign language. Be creative. How can you worship the Lord today?

LORD, I DON'T KNOW ENOUGH WORDS TO TELL YOU HOW AMAZING YOU ARE. BUT HERE ARE A FEW—WONDERFUL, MAGNIFICENT, ALL-POWERFUL, FABULOUS, MARVELOUS. THAT'S WHO YOU ARE! AMEN.

76

ROLLING AROUND ON THE MOON

Serve the Lord with all your heart.

ROMANS 12:11 ICB

BEFORE THE NEXT PERSON takes a step on the Moon, there'll be a whole crew rolling around up there. A crew of robot rovers, that is. They come in all shapes and sizes and from a bunch of different countries. Each one will be able to do something that none of the other robots will be able to do. Some will study the soil and regolith (REG-uh-lith; that's the top layer of dust and rocks). Others will map the Moon's surface, study its magnetics, and look for underground water. They range from NASA's eight-foot-tall VIPER rover to Mexico's one-inch swarm of five robots. These tiny guys are designed to study the Moon's dust. Japanese engineers are even working on a rover that will be able to change shape—like a Transformers toy!

These rovers were all designed to work on the Moon, but each in its own special way. Kind of like us. We were each designed to work—or *serve*—here on Earth. And God gave each of us unique talents to do that. But you've probably heard that before. Here's something you might not have heard. Serving others is one of the greatest cures for loneliness. How? Because it takes our minds off ourselves and makes us think about others instead. It helps us feel useful and needed. And since serving others and showing them God's love is a way to worship Him, it draws us closer to God. Serving also brings other people into our lives, both the people we're serving and the ones we're serving with. Which means it can be a great way to make new friends!

DID YOU KNOW?

NASA has designed a team of shoebox-sized robots called Cooperative Autonomous Distributed Robotic Explorers, or CADRE for short. The plan is for four of these robots to work together to map the Moon's surface. One day, CADRE robots may be sent to map out Mars—or even Jupiter's moons!

GOD, WHEN I'M FEELING LONELY, REMIND ME TO LOOK AROUND FOR THOSE I CAN SERVE AND HELP. AMEN.

77

SMALLER MISSIONS

"Whoever can be trusted with small things can also be trusted with large things."

LUKE 16:10 ICB

WANT TO FLY TO Mars for a year—or at least pretend to? That's what four astronauts will be doing here on Earth. Three separate missions are planned during the 2020s. The crew members will live and work in a habitat like the one NASA plans to use on Mars. It's called Mars Dune Alpha. The astronauts will stay inside and pretend to be on Mars for an entire year!

NASA will study how the astronauts handle the stress of being in a small space, with the same people, for months at a time. The astronauts will use

virtual reality to go on spacewalks—kind of like the video games we play. They'll practice growing their own food, preparing meals, and just generally living, working, and sleeping. This smaller mission will help NASA prepare future astronauts for the much bigger mission to Mars.

Sometimes God gives us smaller missions too. Like helping a friend. Being kind and patient with your brothers and sisters (which, honestly, can seem like a big mission sometimes). Or doing the easy chores your parents tell you to do. These smaller missions help us get ready for the bigger ones. And the better we get at small missions, the more God will trust us with bigger missions. Like helping people we don't know who've been hurt by storms or disasters. Being kind and patient with our enemies. And obeying God even when we don't understand what He's doing.

Whatever mission God has planned for you today—big or small—remember that loving and following Him is the greatest mission of all!

DID YOU KNOW?

Mars Dune Alpha was actually printed out using a 3D printer! It's seventeen hundred square feet, or about the size of a house. It has a kitchen, bedrooms, and bathrooms. But it also has a medical area and a workout room and has space for growing crops and storing robots!

GOD, HELP ME TO SEE EVERY MOMENT AS PART OF A MISSION TO LOVE YOU. AND THANK YOU FOR GOING WITH ME ON EVERY MISSION WE TAKE. AMEN.

78

SPACE VACATION

You have been saved by grace because you believe.
You did not save yourselves. It was a gift from God.

EPHESIANS 2:8 ICB

IF YOU COULD GO anywhere on vacation, where would you go? The beach, the mountains, or an amusement park packed with roller coasters? How about outer space? That's what a billionaire from California did! In 2001, Dennis Tito became the first space tourist when he hitched a ride to the International Space Station (ISS) on board a Russian Soyuz rocket. His "ticket" cost $20 million! That bought him an eight-day stay on the ISS, where he orbited the Earth 128 times! How did it feel? "Absolutely euphoric," he said. (*Euphoric* [yoo-FOR-ik] means, "This is the best thing ever!") As he looked out through space and back to the Earth, Tito said to himself, "I've done it. I'm in space."[23]

Here's the thing, though. Tito didn't do it. Yes, he trained with Russian cosmonauts (that's what Russian astronauts are called). Yes, he rode the rocket into space. And yes, he paid a huge price for the trip. But he didn't get himself there. A rocket, thousands of space experts, and other cosmonauts got him there.

Just like Tito couldn't get himself into space, we can't get ourselves to heaven. We can't buy a ticket. And we can't be perfect enough to get there on our own, no matter how much we train. We need someone to make a way: Jesus. He came from heaven to show us how to live and love God. Then He died on the cross, taking the punishment for all our sins. And when He rose up from the grave and went up to heaven again, Jesus opened the way for us to get to heaven too. How? By trusting that He really is God's Son. By obeying Him. And if you mess up, by asking Him to forgive you. He will because that's His gift to you. It's called *grace*. And Jesus' grace is the only thing that gets us to heaven.

DID YOU KNOW?

In 2022, three more space tourists headed up to the International Space Station. They traveled with a trained astronaut in the SpaceX Dragon spacecraft and stayed for ten days on board the ISS. Each "ticket" cost $55 million! But the food was free, and the view was out of this world!

GOD, THANK YOU FOR JESUS. THANK YOU FOR GRACE. THANK YOU FOR WANTING TO BE WITH ME FOREVER. AMEN.

79

TRASH TALK

Always be willing to listen and slow to speak.

JAMES 1:19 ICB

TRASH ON MARS? PEOPLE haven't even landed there yet, but there's already about seven tons of trash on Mars. How did it get there? From the fourteen different missions to Mars that countries around the world have launched over the past fifty years.

No, Mars isn't littered with straw wrappers or plastic cups. Instead, bits and pieces of heat shields—the stuff that protects spacecraft from burning up as they zoom through Mars's atmosphere—are scattered across the surface. Parachutes and landing gear snag on rocks and fall into craters. And, of course, the spacecraft themselves—at least nine have either crashed or stopped working—collect dust on the Red Planet. Even the Perseverance rover is a litter bug. It landed on Mars in 2021 and soon after dropped a piece of its drill. All that trash gets blown around by Martian winds. It can tangle up rovers and mess up the samples they collect. It could even threaten future missions.

Space litter isn't the only kind of troublesome trash, though. Our words can be trouble too. If we toss them out without thinking before we speak, talk can cause big trouble. Thoughtless words can slip out when we're angry, in a hurry, or just not listening to what the other person is saying. They can hurt feelings and ruin friendships. So let's slow down and choose our words carefully. Let's *THINK*! That is, use the letters of the word *THINK* to guide your words before you speak.

DID YOU KNOW?

Some of that trash on Mars is actually useful. Like the parachute from Perseverance. Over time, Martian dust will cover its bright colors, and that will help scientists learn about the weather and windspeeds on Mars.

T: Is it true?

H: Is it helpful?

I: Will it inspire or injure?

N: It is necessary to say?

K: Is it kind?

Toss the trash talk and *THINK* before you speak!

LORD, PLEASE HELP ME NOT TO LITTER THE WORLD AROUND ME WITH THOUGHTLESS WORDS. I WANT MY WORDS TO BE TRUE AND HELPFUL— NOT TRASH! AMEN.

80

RING AROUND . . . NEPTUNE?

A friend loves you all the time.

PROVERBS 17:17 ICB

RING AND *PLANET.* WHEN you hear those two words, which planet do you think of? Saturn, right? That's because Saturn's rings shine bold and bright! Saturn isn't the only planet in our solar system with rings, though. Neptune has rings too, along with Jupiter and Uranus! Astronomers have known that for a while. But because Neptune is 2.8 billion miles from the Sun, we don't know a lot about its rings.

But we do know that Neptune has five main rings, along with a few lighter ones. Astronomers believe the rings are mostly made of icy dust. In 2022, they were at last able to get a closer look. That's when the super-powerful James Webb Space Telescope (JWST) sent some pictures back to NASA showing off

Neptune's stack of rings. (Learn more about the JWST on page 172.) The JWST's pictures of Neptune's rings are the first astronomers have seen since the Voyager 2 spacecraft zipped past Neptune in 1989. Scientists are still studying the pictures, but they're hoping to learn a lot more about the rings of this less-popular but oh-so-amazing planet.

Friendships can be kind of like the rings of Saturn and Neptune. It's easy to notice the popular kids. They shine bold and bright! And if we're not careful, we might start to think they'd be better friends. We can even end up doing some pretty silly things to try to be part of their crowd. True friends—whether they're popular or not—are the ones who care about you all the time, no matter what clothes you wear, no matter what sports you play, and no matter if people think you're cool or not. Forget about popularity and focus on finding true friends. They're the ones who'll encourage you to love others and God. And they'll help you be a true friend too.

DID YOU KNOW?

Neptune is so far from the Sun that temperatures average a freezing –373 degrees Fahrenheit, and its fastest winds whip through at 1,200 miles per hour. Compare that to Earth's coldest temperature of –128.6 degrees Fahrenheit (recorded in Antarctica). Even Earth's fastest tornado clocked in at *only* 302 miles per hour!

FATHER, SOMETIMES I THINK BEING POPULAR WOULD MAKE MY LIFE SO MUCH EASIER AND BETTER. HELP ME TO LOOK FOR TRUE FRIENDS INSTEAD—AND TO BE A TRUE FRIEND TOO. AMEN.

81

NO MATTER HOW BIG, NO MATTER HOW SMALL

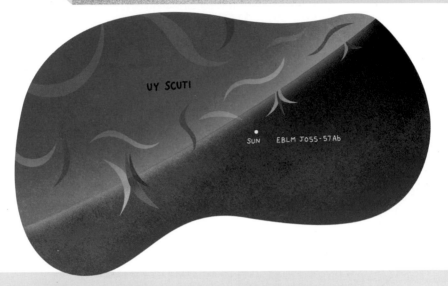

Give all your worries to him, because he cares for you.

1 PETER 5:7 ICB

A STAR IS A STAR. They're all the same, right? *Wrong!* Those twinkly lights might look alike from down here on Earth. But get a little closer, and you'll discover that stars come in all different sizes. Our Sun is huge from our perspective; you could fit 1.3 million Earths inside it. But it is only a medium-sized star. The biggest star astronomers have found so far is UY Scuti. It's a red hypergiant, which means it looks red and, well, it's *really* big. You could fit about five billion Suns inside of it! If you could stuff stars into stars, that is. To give you a sense of its size, consider this: if our Sun were a gumball, UY Scuti would be a building ten stories tall!

Then there's the tiniest star: EBLM J0555–57Ab. (It really needs a better name. Maybe Teeny or Wee-Star.) Scientists discovered EBLM in 2017—over six hundred light-years away from Earth. It's about the size of Saturn and so tiny it barely qualifies as a star. About 1,700 EBLMs would fit inside our Sun!

Whether big or small, God knows every single star (Psalm 147:4)—just like He knows every single one of your worries and struggles. Now, you might think, *It's just a quiz. I shouldn't bother God with it.* Or *God has got more important stuff to take care of.* Or maybe you think, *It's no big deal. I can handle it by myself.* But God wants to hear about and help you through *all* your struggles. So tell Him about the school assignment that is late and the shoe you can't find. Talk to Him when you're feeling blue and don't know why. Because life is just better when you share it with the One who counts the stars.

DID YOU KNOW?

Scientists believe there are at least 100 billion stars in the Milky Way galaxy and billions of other galaxies full of billions of stars in the universe. What's the *universe*? It's everything in space—galaxies, stars, planets, asteroids, and anything else we discover! And how big is it? No one knows. Except God, of course!

GOD, THANK YOU FOR LISTENING TO MY TROUBLES. TODAY, I'M STRUGGLING WITH _____. AMEN.

82

THE EDGE OF THE UNIVERSE

He made the sun and the moon. His love continues forever.

PSALM 136:7 ICB

YOU'VE BEEN TO THE edge of your town. You might have walked along the edge of the ocean. But imagine seeing the edge of the *universe*! That's the mission of the James Webb Space Telescope—or JWST for short.

The JWST is the biggest and most powerful space telescope ever built. It's as tall as a three-story building and as wide as a tennis court! How did something so huge get into space? Engineers folded it up like origami inside the rocket and launched it on Christmas Day, December 25, 2021. It traveled for thirty days to a spot almost a million miles away called the Lagrange Point 2.

The JWST will stay there, orbiting the Sun, for the next twenty years or so.

With its huge mirror—over twenty-one feet across—the JWST is sending back pictures from the edge of the universe. Just how far away is that edge? Some scientists think it could be over *93 billion light-years* away! Others, like Albert Einstein, believe the universe never ends! That means it is infinite (IN-fuh-nit)—without a beginning or an end. (Mind-blowing, right?)

Want to know what else is infinite? The One who made the universe: God. He has no beginning and no end. (Definitely mind-blowing!) God has always been and will always be. His love for you is infinite too. It has always been and will always be. Nothing you ever do will make Him stop loving you (Romans 8:38–39). And nothing could make Him love you more. You don't have to earn His love or prove yourself. You don't have to "try out" for His team, get everything right, or know the answer to every Bible trivia question. God loves you. Period. How marvelous is that?

DID YOU KNOW?

Scientists often measure distances in space with light-years. That's how far light travels in a year. Light travels at 186,000 miles per second. So in a year, it can travel about 5.88 trillion miles—that's 5,880,000,000,000 miles! Even if you could travel at the speed of light, it would still take you 4.6 hours to get to Pluto! And that's not even leaving the "front porch" of this marvelous universe God has made for us.

GOD, THANK YOU FOR LOVING ME NO MATTER WHAT I DO. AMEN.

83

BETWEEN THE STARS

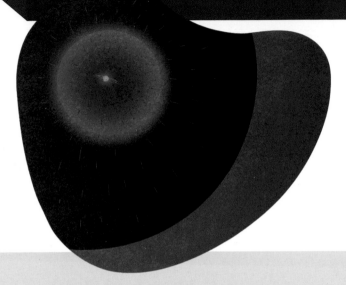

> If I rise with the sun in the east, and settle in the west beyond the sea, even there you would guide me. With your right hand you would hold me.

PSALM 139:9–10 ICB

WE'VE ALL HEARD OF *outer* space, but *interstellar* space? What's that? The easy answer is, it's the space between stars. But it's actually a little more complicated than that—and it all has to do with our Sun.

The Sun is constantly pushing its magnetic field and particles out into the space around it. This creates a *solar wind* that travels at over 670,000 miles per hour. The area the solar wind touches is like a giant bubble called the

heliosphere (HEE-lee-uh-sfeer). It stretches way out past Pluto. The area outside the solar wind's reach is called the *heliopause* (HEE-lee-uh-pawz)—or interstellar space. It begins roughly eleven billion (that's 11,000,000,000) miles from the Sun!

Imagine leaving the bubble of everything scientists know and adventuring out into interstellar space! That might not happen anytime soon, but there are some "bubbles" you can leave right here on Earth. Like the bubble of always hanging out with the same friends or talking to people you already know at church. Don't be afraid to branch out and include new people in your friend group. There's also the "bubble" of always doing the same things and eating the same foods. Pop those bubbles by trying something new— like in-line skating, tumbling, painting, or whatever sounds interesting to you. Try some sushi or stir-fry or brussels sprouts. Sure, it can be a little risky. You might not like everything you try. You'll need to be brave to try new things and meet new people. So try memorizing a verse like Joshua 1:9 or Psalm 28:7—they'll remind you that God will help you be brave.

There's a great big world out there just waiting to be discovered. Be bold, step out of your "bubble," and try something new.

GOD, HELP ME TO BE BRAVE TO BEFRIEND NEW PEOPLE AND TRY NEW THINGS. AMEN.

DID YOU KNOW?

Only two spacecraft—so far!—have traveled into interstellar space: the unmanned Voyager 1 and Voyager 2. They've been traveling since 1977, and they are still sending back data for NASA to study!

84

A SYMPHONY IN SPACE

"The mountains and hills will burst into song before you. All the trees in the fields will clap their hands."

ISAIAH 55:12 ICB

ON EARTH, WE CAN step out into nature and hear all sorts of sounds. Birds chirping, leaves rustling, and bugs buzzing by. But if you could step "out" into space, what would you hear?

Telescopes allow us to see pictures of space and all its stars and planets. But NASA's scientists wanted to turn those pictures into sounds, or "sonify" (SAHN-ih-fye) them. This would let members of the blind community "see" space too. So they assigned the data from each space telescope—the Chandra X-ray, the Hubble, the James Webb, and the Spitzer—a different instrument or set of instruments (like brass trumpets, string violins, and woodwind clarinets). Bright spots in the pictures were made louder, while the color and position of

objects in the pictures controlled how high or low the pitch was. The results are amazing! (Ask your parents to help you check them out at www.chandra.si.edu/sound/.) It's a symphony in space!

Right now, we can hear little bits of the music of God's creation on Earth. But one day Jesus will return, and the curse of sin will be lifted away. No more death or disease, not even for the animals or trees. Instead, we'll hear a perfect "symphony" of this world—without any sounds of crying or anger or hurting. Everything will be made perfect again, just as God created it to be. And the air will be filled with all the beautiful sounds of God's creation, like waterfalls and birds singing. We might even hear the trees clapping for Jesus, our King!

Until then, step outside, close your eyes, and listen for God's creation. Can you hear it "sing"? Imagine how wonderful the song will be when Jesus comes again!

LORD, THANK YOU FOR MY EYES THAT SEE AND MY EARS THAT HEAR. TEACH ME TO LOOK AND LISTEN TO THE SYMPHONY OF YOUR CREATION. AMEN.

DID YOU KNOW?

We can sometimes "taste" the air on Earth— especially when it's about to rain or snow. What about space? What does space taste like? Raspberries! Or at least part of it does. Scientists used a process called *spectroscopy* (spek-TRAH-skuh-pee) to test a giant cloud of space dust in the middle of the Milky Way. They found ethyl formate—a chemical that gives raspberries their "raspberry" taste!

85

A GALACTIC CRASH!

Do what is right to other people. Love being kind to others. And live humbly, trusting your God.

MICAH 6:8 ICB

WHAT WOULD HAPPEN IF two galaxies crashed into each other? That's the question you might ask after seeing a recent picture from the Hubble Space Telescope. The picture shows two galaxies that look like they're slamming into each other! The two galaxies are called SDSS J115331 and LEDA 2073461. (Seriously, somebody needs to come up with better names!) These two galaxies are more than a billion light-years away from Earth. But astronomers believe the two galaxies aren't really touching at all. Most likely, they're just cruising by each other in the vastness of space.

Sometimes it can feel like our worlds are crashing into each other. Like when a kid from school walks into your church. Or your Sunday school teacher shows up at your ball game. Or you bump into a teacher while you're out to dinner with your family. It can feel a little weird, especially if you've been acting different ways with different groups. Maybe you've been doing whatever it takes to fit in with the cool kids at school, or you've been talking trash at ball games—but then acting extra "good" at home and church. If *who you are* changes depending on *who you're with*, you'll have all kinds of problems when those different worlds crash into each other.

It's so easy to avoid that whole crashing thing, though. Just be the same person no matter where you go or who you're with. And who is that person? God gives us some great examples in Micah 6:8. Check it out!

DID YOU KNOW?

What happens when galaxies actually do crash into each other? Well, thankfully, they don't really crash. It's more of a *whoosh* sound. They just sort of merge together over millions of years. Planets and moons get moved around. Orbits change. And stars— sometimes thousands of them—are born!

GOD, HELP ME TO BE THE SAME PERSON WHEREVER I GO AND WHOEVER I'M WITH—SOMEONE WHO LOVES YOU! AMEN.

86

TOO HOT TO HANDLE!

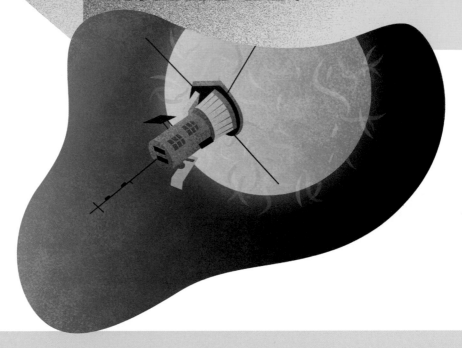

When a wise person sees danger ahead, he avoids it.

PROVERBS 27:12 ICB

THE PARKER SOLAR PROBE is on a mission—*to touch the Sun!* Since 2018, it's been orbiting, or looping, around the Sun and out past Venus. With each orbit, Parker gets closer and closer to the Sun. During its final three orbits, it will get *really* close—only 3.83 million miles from the Sun. (That might not seem close, but Earth is 93 million miles from the Sun.) Parker will then be traveling at about 430,000 miles per hour. The temperatures on its front solar shields (the ones facing the Sun) will reach about 2,600 degrees Fahrenheit, but the back of the craft will only be about eighty-five degrees.

Scientists are hoping Parker will help them learn more about solar winds and the Sun's corona (kuh-ROH-nuh), or super-hot atmosphere. No other spacecraft has ever gotten this close to the Sun, because it's just too hot to handle!

One day, you may find yourself stuck in a situation that's too hot to handle. You could be hanging out with friends who start making bad choices. Or you might start to feel uncomfortable at a party or sleepover, and you just need to go home without making a big deal out of it. *Before* any of that happens, sit down with your parents and come up with a code word or phrase, like "My stomach hurts" or "I've got homework." Then, if you call or text and use those words, your parents will know to come get you right away. No questions asked. Be wise and be ready with a plan *before* things get too hot to handle.

GOD, GIVE ME THE WISDOM TO KNOW WHEN I'M SOMEWHERE I SHOULDN'T BE. AND GIVE ME THE COURAGE TO LEAVE. AMEN.

DID YOU KNOW?

Why won't the Parker Solar Probe melt? Because even though the particles of the Sun's corona are moving incredibly fast, there aren't that many of them. Fewer particles means that they don't bump into each other—and the Parker Solar Probe—as often. And it's that bumping that causes heat. So while temperatures in the corona will reach more than three million degrees Fahrenheit, the Parker itself won't get hot enough to melt!

87

NOT A DINOSAUR

**That is how much God loved us, dear friends!
So we also must love each other.**

1 JOHN 4:11 ICB

THE OSIRIS-REX IS NOT a newly discovered species of dinosaur—no matter what its name sounds like. It's a spacecraft that launched back in 2016. After traveling two years and a few million miles, it finally reached its target: the asteroid Bennu (BEH-noo). OSIRIS-REx then spent the next two years orbiting around Bennu and studying its surface. It even did a quick landing to scoop up some samples of rocks and dirt!

Scientists have already learned some surprising things about Bennu. Like its surface. Scientists expected it to be smooth and sandy. Instead, it was rocky, jagged, and covered with boulders. And the spot where OSIRIS-REx needed to land wasn't solid at all. It was more like a plastic ball pit you would find in a play place. No kidding! OSIRIS-REx had to fire its thrusters to keep from sinking in. One scientist said, "Our expectations about the asteroid's surface were completely wrong."[24]

Expectations (ek-spek-TAY-shuhnz) are what we *think* will happen. But things don't always turn out the way we think they will. Sometimes our expectations are completely wrong, just like those scientists' expectations about the surface of Bennu. So what do you do when a friendship doesn't go the way you expect it to? Like when you find out that the person you just *knew* would be your new friend doesn't like any of the same things you do? Well, one thing you don't do is give up on the possibility of a friendship. Then ask God to help you sort it out. Sure, it might be a little awkward, but pretend you're on a scientific exploration. Ask questions and try to find out all you can about the other person. What does she like? What's his favorite ice cream? What are the things she likes to do? Every person is a fascinating creation of God. And the more you learn, the better your chances of discovering something you both enjoy—like dinosaurs or space travel and, of course, God!

GOD, HELP ME TO SEE EVERY PERSON AS SOMEONE WORTH LEARNING MORE ABOUT. AMEN.

DID YOU KNOW?

Another spacecraft is on its way to another asteroid—actually a bunch of asteroids. This spacecraft is named Lucy. It launched in 2021 on a twelve-year mission to study the Trojan asteroids. These asteroids are grouped together around Jupiter. One bunch travels in front of Jupiter as it orbits the Sun, and the other group follows after. Lucy will explore more asteroids than any other spacecraft!

88

TARANTULAS IN SPACE?!

By faith we understand that the universe was created by the word of God.

HEBREWS 11:3 ESV

A **TARANTULA IN SPACE?! WELL,** not exactly. The Tarantula Nebula (NEB-yuh-luh) is the nickname for the 30 Doradus (duh-RAY-duhs)—a sort of star nursery where stars are born. It's called the Tarantula Nebula because pictures from older telescopes kind of look like a spider's legs are sticking out of a "dusty" cluster of stars. It's 161,000 light-years away, so getting a clear picture isn't easy! Then, in 2021, along came the incredibly powerful James Webb Space Telescope (JWST). For the first time ever, scientists were able to see behind all that "star dust." (Learn more about the JWST on page 172.)

Instead of dust, the JWST's pictures showed scientists thousands of stars they'd never seen before. They also got a glimpse of other galaxies in the background. They even saw a star being formed! The JWST is just getting started with its picture taking, so imagine all the discoveries it will make! There will be no end because there's no end to God and His creation.

We might not know all there is to know about the universe, but there is one thing we *do* know: God is so big and so powerful that He can hold the whole thing in His hands! He knows every star, every planet, every moon, and every nebula in it. He also knows every answer to every question you could ever ask— about the universe, our troubles, or how to deal with the kid who likes to tease you. When you need answers, turn to God—by praying, reading His Word, and talking to others who love Him. Because God knows everything!

DID YOU KNOW?

Scientists say the James Webb Space Telescope is the most powerful telescope ever built. Just how powerful is it? If the JWST were still here on Earth, it could sense the body heat of a bumblebee all the way on the Moon! With your parents' permission, check out some of the amazing pictures the JWST is sending back to Earth at www.webbtelescope.org. They are marvelous!

GOD, THERE ARE SO MANY QUESTIONS I HAVEN'T EVEN THOUGHT TO ASK YET, AND YOU ALREADY KNOW THE ANSWER TO THEM ALL! YOU'RE AMAZING! AMEN.

89

ENDLESS DISCOVERY

The heavens tell the glory of God. And the skies announce what his hands have made.

PSALM 19:1 ICB

I**T'S ONE OF THE** world's largest, most powerful telescopes, and it has an amazing name. You'll never guess it. It's called the (drum roll, please) . . . Very Large Telescope! No, seriously. That's what it's called. The Very Large Telescope (VLT) was built by the European Southern Observatory—or ESO—in the Atacama Desert of Chile. It began operating in

1999. The VLT is actually made up of four larger telescopes and four smaller ones. These telescopes can be used separately. But when they all work together, they make a telescope so powerful that it could "see" the headlights of a car on the Moon (roughly 240,000 miles away). The VLT has tracked stars moving around a black hole in the Milky Way, and it's even snapped the first image of an exoplanet—that's a planet that doesn't orbit our Sun.

Thousands of years ago, David stood out in the fields of Bethlehem, watching over his father's sheep and staring up at the same universe of stars that we see. David probably never imagined all the wonders we would one day see with technology like the VLT. But David did know two very important things—and those two things will never change. First, God is the One who hung all the stars in the sky. And second, we will never be alone—because He will always be with us.

LORD, TODAY, PLEASE HELP ME TO LEARN ONE MORE THING ABOUT HOW AWESOME YOU ARE. AMEN.

DID YOU KNOW?

As amazing as the Very Large Telescope is, the ESO is building an even bigger one. It'll be the Earth's largest telescope. And guess what it'll be called—the Extremely Large Telescope! It's being built high on a mountain in the Atacama Desert in Chile. Called the ELT for short, it's expected to be finished in 2027. It will study and search for exoplanets, black holes, and other galaxies in the universe. You don't need an ELT to count the stars. Just spread a blanket outside, away from lights, and snuggle up with your parents. As your eyes get used to the dark, you'll see more and more stars!

90

THE ULTIMATE MISSION

Mercury 7 of Project Mercury

I praise you because of the wonderful way you created me. Everything you do is marvelous!

PSALM 139:14 CEV

OCTOBER 1, 1958—THAT'S THE DAY NASA (short for National Aeronautics and Space Administration) officially started. For more than sixty years, they've been studying space and figuring out ways to explore it. One of their first projects, Project Mercury, was just to see if humans could survive in space. Project Gemini studied what they would need to land on the Moon. And the Apollo projects finally put people on the Moon. But NASA didn't stop there. They launched satellites and massive telescopes.

They sent a probe to the Sun and a rover to Mars. They're carrying out the mission they were created for: "NASA explores the unknown in air and space, innovates for the benefit of humanity, and inspires the world through discovery."[25]

You have a mission, too, and it's an amazing mission. As a child of God, you were made to dream, imagine, explore, and discover. In your home and school, in your city and church, in the world, and maybe even beyond this world. And you were made to do all of that *with God*. There's no end to all the wonders He can show you.

Your mission won't look like anyone else's because God didn't create anyone else like you. But your mission will be just as wonderful. So don't be afraid to be who He created you to be—wonderful, unique, and maybe even a little weird in the most marvelous of ways. In fact, the more you discover who God created you to be and the more you explore God's marvelous creation, the more you'll be ready for the ultimate mission of all time: to live your life loving God and helping others to love Him too! Are you ready for your mission? If so, come on! It's time to get set and blastoff!

GET READY TO MARVEL!

God's given you some objectives (or goals) for your life's mission. Want to know what they are? Check out these verses to find the answers: Matthew 22:37, Matthew 22:39, Matthew 28:19, and Mark 16:15. Once you know your objectives, then you are a "go" for launch into a life lived with and for God!

GOD, I BELIEVE THAT YOU HAVE A MISSION PLANNED JUST FOR ME—AND I'M READY FOR THE ADVENTURE! AMEN.

NOTES

1. Mike Wall, "JFK's 'Moon Speech' Still Resonates 50 Years Later," Space.com, September 12, 2012, https://www.space.com/17547-jfk-moon-speech-50years-anniversary.html.
2. "Astronaut Alan B. Shepard, Jr., May 5, 1961," NASA, last updated August 7, 2017, https://www.nasa.gov/multimedia/imagegallery/image_feature_1076.html.
3. Elizabeth Howell, "Astronaut Alan Shepard's Daughter Says She's Excited to Follow Him to Space," Space.com, December 10, 2021, https://www.space.com/alan-shepard-daughter-laura-excited-space.
4. Julie Zauzmer, "In Space, John Glenn Saw the Face of God: 'It Just Strengthens My Faith,'" *Washington Post*, December 8, 2016, https://www.washingtonpost.com/news/acts-of-faith/wp/2016/12/08/in-outer-space-john-glenn-saw-the-face-of-god/.
5. Mark Wolverton, "The G Machine," *Smithsonian Magazine*, May 2007, https://www.smithsonianmag.com/air-space-magazine/the-g-machine-16799374/.
6. International Center of Photography, "[Edward Higgins White's Space Walk]," from The *LIFE* Magazine Collection, 2005, https://www.icp.org/browse/archive/objects/edward-higgins-whites-space-walk.
7. Ibid.
8. "July 20, 1969: One Giant Leap for Mankind," NASA, July 20, 2019, https://www.nasa.gov/mission_pages/apollo/apollo11.html.
9. Yvette Smith, ed., "Celebrating the Life and Career of Katherine Johnson," NASA, February 24, 2020, https://www.nasa.gov/image-feature/celebrating-the-life-and-career-of-katherine-johnson.
10. Lance Eliot, "Apollo 11's Infamous Landing Error Code 1202 Offers Earthly Lessons for Self-Driving Cars," *Forbes*, July 16, 2019, https://www.forbes.com/sites/lanceeliot/2019/07/16/apollo-11s-infamous-landing-error-code-1202-offers-earthly-lessons-for-self-driving-cars/?sh=7595815034bc.
11. "July 20, 1969: One Giant Leap for Mankind," NASA, July 20, 2019, https://www.nasa.gov/mission_pages/apollo/apollo11.html.
12. "Fact Sheet: Apollo 11 35th Anniversary," George W. Bush White House Archives, July 20, 2004, https://georgewbush-whitehouse.archives.gov/news/releases/2004/07/20040720-8.html.
13. "The Eagle Has Landed, the Flight of Apollo 11, 1969 (excerpt)," US National Archives, July 19, 2019, YouTube video, 2:01, https://www.youtube.com/watch?v=himJ4LuO0hI.
14. "Astronaut Friday: Neil Armstrong," Space Center Houston, August 16, 2019, https://spacecenter.org/astronaut-friday-neil-armstrong/.
15. Jessie Kratz, "Two Generations of Flight and One Historic Mission," *Pieces of History* (blog), US National Archives, November 30, 2018, https://prologue.blogs.archives.gov/2018/11/30/two-generations-of-flight-and-one-historic-mission/.
16. John Uri, "Fifty Years Ago: Apollo 13 Off to the Moon," *Roundup Reads* (blog), NASA, April 9, 2020, https://roundupreads.jsc.nasa.gov/roundup/1402/Fifty%20Years%20Ago%20Apollo%2013%20Off%20to%20the%20Moon.
17. Christian Davenport, "'We Shall Return': Eugene Cernan Was the Last Man to Walk on the Moon. There Was No Return," *Washington Post*, December 14, 2017, https://www.washingtonpost.com/news/retropolis/wp/2017/12/14/we-shall-return-eugene-cernan-was-the-last-man-to-walk-on-the-moon-there-was-no-return/.
18. Ben Evans, "Ride, Sally Ride: 35 Years Since America's First Woman in Space," AmericaSpace, June 17, 2018, https://www.americaspace.com/2018/06/17/ride-sally-ride-35-years-since-americas-first-woman-in-space/.
19. Brian Anderson, "Innovator's Spotlight: Col. Guion S. Bluford," Air Force, April 16, 2021, https://www.af.mil/News/Article-Display/Article/2575707/innovators-spotlight-col-guion-s-bluford/.
20. Gillian Jacobs, "Astronaut Peggy Whitson Is Breaking Records and Pushing the Boundaries for Women in Space," *Glamour*, October 30, 2017, https://www.glamour.com/story/women-of-the-year-2017-peggy-whitson.
21. Levi Lusko, *The Last Supper on the Moon* (Nashville: Thomas Nelson, 2022), xi.
22. Alaina, "Snoopy, Charlie Brown and Apollo 10," *The Payload Blog*, Kennedy Space Center, May 16, 2019, https://www.kennedyspacecenter.com/blog/snoopy-charlie-brown-and-apollo-10.
23. Jim Clash, "Wilshire Associates Founder Dennis Tito Reflects on His Rare Spaceflight," *Forbes*, March 27, 2017, https://www.forbes.com/sites/jimclash/2017/03/27/wilshire-associates-founder-dennis-tito-reflects-on-his-rare-spaceflight/?sh=1463d06c64f7.
24. Svetlana Shekhtman, "NASA Reveals Surface of Asteroid Bennu Is like Plastic Ball Pit," NASA, July 6, 2022, https://www.nasa.gov/feature/goddard/2022/surprise-again-asteroid-bennu-reveals-its-surface-is-like-a-plastic-ball-pit.
25. NASA, "Our Missions and Values," April 15, 2022, https://www.nasa.gov/careers/our-mission-and-values.

ABOUT THE AUTHOR

LEVI LUSKO is the founder and lead pastor of Fresh Life Church located in Montana, Idaho, Oregon, and Utah. He is the bestselling author of *Through the Eyes of a Lion*, *Swipe Right*, *I Declare War*, *The Last Supper on the Moon*, and *Roar Like a Lion*, the 2022 ECPA Christian Book Award winner for young people's literature. Levi also travels the world speaking about Jesus. He and his wife, Jennie, have one son, Lennox, and four daughters: Alivia, Daisy, Clover, and Lenya, who is in heaven.

ABOUT THE ILLUSTRATORS

CATHERINE PEARSON is a Swiss illustrator based in the hills of Lausanne, Switzerland. With a European bachelor's degree in illustration, Catherine, through her career and experiences, has refined a unique and playful illustration style. She is passionate about bringing clients' ideas to life and believes illustration can speak to you where words cannot. Her sharp eye for color and composition brings a unique and striking originality.

    TIM BRADFORD has a master's degree in illustration and animation from Kingston University in London. He is known for the versatility of his character designs and ability to make each art piece into something unique and vibrant. His clients include Shell, Ford, Microsoft, HarperCollins, and more. Tim currently lives next to a nature reserve in Nottingham, England.

HOW MANY TELESCOPES DID YOU FIND?

TELESCOPES HELP US GET a clearer, closer look at the things we can see with our eyes, like the Moon. They also let us see things that we couldn't see with just our eyes—like faraway stars and even other galaxies. And that makes telescopes a lot like faith. How? Because just like those faraway galaxies, we can't see God with our eyes. But we can "see" Him by faith when we look up at the night sky and this universe that He's created (Hebrews 11:1; Romans 1:20). And like a telescope, faith gives a clearer look at the world around us that we *can* see. When we look through the "telescope" of faith, we see that God is always with us and always busy helping us. So the next time you feel nervous or afraid or alone, pull up your faith like a telescope and "see" how God is busy helping you.

To help you remember to look at the world through the telescope of faith, there are 19 telescopes hidden throughout the illustrations in this book (not including the ones on the introduction and this page). How many did you find? Here's where they are hidden: pages 12, 16, 24, 26, 48, 66, 74, 76, 86, 88, 94, 96, 116, 124, 142, 156, 160, 164, 166.

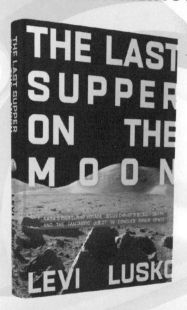